TOURISM

Robin Walker and Keith Harding

Student's Book

OXFORD
UNIVERSITY PRESS

Contents

1 Arrivals

Take off

Look at the photos.

1 Where are they?

EXAMPLE *at a hotel*

2 What type of tourist or visitor is being welcomed in each case?

Reading

Welcome – the first encounter

1 Match the words with their dictionary definitions.

1 encounter 3 hospitality
2 experience 4 welcome

a friendly and generous behaviour towards guests
b a meeting, especially one that is sudden and unexpected
c a greeting that is given to somebody when they arrive, especially a friendly one
d something that has happened to you, often unusual or exciting

2 Read the text. Which subtitle do you think is the best?

- Tourism: the encounters industry
- Tourism: the experience industry
- Tourism: the hospitality industry
- Tourism: the welcome industry

3 Which of the six points (a–f) would include this advice?

1 Offer to carry a bag, to get a drink, to open the door, anything to show you're there to help.
2 Do your research – know who you're meeting, know where you're going.
3 Have confidence in your abilities and personality.
4 There are many ways of greeting in different countries, but the smile is universal.
5 Dress appropriately – be smart, clean, and tidy.
6 Find out about the person you're with, and ask them about themselves.

4 Can you think of more advice to add to the list above?

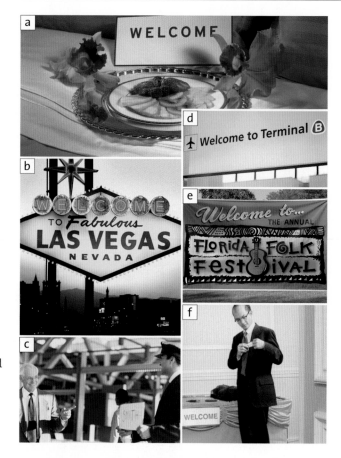

An introduction to working in tourism

Tourism is about encounters – encounters with people, with places, and with experiences. And the most important encounter is the first one: arrival and greetings. Get that one right and the rest is much easier.

Arrival encounters can take place anywhere: at the airport, at the hotel, at the campsite, in the restaurant, on the tour bus, or at the attraction. Wherever it takes place, the rules are the same:

a Be prepared   d Be interested
b Look the part   e Be helpful
c Smile   f Be yourself.

In this unit
- welcoming
- greeting and introducing
- car hire
- describing arrival services

Where in the world?

What do you know about Singapore?

1 Is it an island or on the mainland?

2 Where is it located?

3 Why do tourists visit Singapore and where do they come from?

Read on and find out.

A warm welcome to the world's most colourful city – Singapore

An exciting tropical destination with modern western comforts and an Asian soul.

Fact file

Location: the Republic of Singapore consists of the island of Singapore and around sixty smaller islands off the southern tip of Malaysia, 135 kilometres north of the equator.

Capital: Singapore City is the country's capital and occupies the main island.

Size: 650 square kilometres

Population: approximately 4.2 million

Tourism

Visitors outnumber the local population by 1.6 to 1.

Visitors come from many countries. The top three are Indonesia (17%), Japan (13%), and Australia (6%). They usually stay for short visits, often stopovers en route to other Asian countries or Australia or New Zealand, or for sightseeing and shopping.

Transport hub

Changi Airport consists of three terminals and is one of the most important air hubs in the region.

The International Airport serves 167 cities in 53 countries and is capable of handling 64 million passengers a year.

Transport from the airport

Number 36 bus to Orchard Road
Maxicab shuttle bus (06.00–24.00)
MRT train (Mass Rapid Transit) (05.30–23.00).

The Port of Singapore is the world's busiest port for cargo, and is also a stopping place for cruise ships.

namaste is the way of greeting in India and some other Asian countries. The word is said with the palms of the hands held together, with fingers pointing up and touching the chin, and with a slight bow.

Customer care

Cultural differences in greetings

Even before you say a word, there are many ways of greeting people. How you do it will depend on many things, for example your nationality and culture, how well you know the person you are greeting, your relative ages, and your gender. You need to think about who you are meeting and greeting before you do it.

1 Do you know what each of these ways of greeting is?

2 Would you use these greetings? In which situation?

3 Which of the greetings in **1** do you associate with the following regions?

- Northern Europe
- Southern Europe
- Eastern Europe
- North America
- Central and South America
- the Middle East
- Africa
- Asia
- Australasia

Listening

Greeting and introducing

1 🎧 Listen to eight greetings and introductions. For each one, answer the questions.

1 Where does the conversation take place?
2 Have the speakers met before?
3 Is the conversation formal or informal?
4 Is another person or are other people introduced?

2 🎧 Listen again and complete the sentences.

1 Hello, Peter – it's _____ again. Welcome to Atlanta. How was your flight?

2 Hello, and _____ joining us tonight. _____ Praphat and _____ my colleague Amphai. We'll _____ on tonight's excursion.

3 Good _____, Mr Ellman. Is everything to _____? _____ get you some more wine?

4 _____ introduce myself? My name is Chie Mashida and I'm the manager. _____ to the people who are going to be looking after you during the conference. _____ Masako …

5 A Hi, it's Johann, _____? Glad you could make it. _____?

   B Good, yeah. You?

   A _____. Have you _____ Lucy? She organized this reception.

6 Ladies and gentlemen, _____ Paradise Cruises, _____ you all on board. We _____ to offer you a complimentary glass of champagne.

7 You _____ Ms Holweger. Welcome to Copenhagen. _____ take your bag for you.

8 Welcome _____, Dr Allegretti. Nice _____. We've put you in your usual room.

Bienvenue
Willkommen
ようこそ
Benvenuto
приветствовать   Üdvözöljük

● Language spot
Greeting and introducing

1 Look at the expressions from *Listening* and add more examples.

Greeting	Welcoming
Hello, Peter – it's great to see you again.	Welcome to Atlanta.

Introducing yourself	Introducing someone else
My name's Praphat.	This is my colleague Amphai.

Checking someone's identity	Making an offer
You must be Ms Holweger.	Can I get you some more wine?

2 Match the following responses with some of the conversations in *Listening* **2**.

a That's very kind. It's rather heavy. Is the car very far?

b It was OK, although it was rather long. Are we going straight to the hotel?

c No, I don't think we've met before. You've done a great job.

d No, thank you, I'm OK. It's very nice though – where's it from?

3 In pairs, practise the conversations. Try to continue the conversations for a few more sentences.

>> Go to **Grammar reference** p.118

Speaking
Welcoming visitors

1 You're meeting a visitor to your country at the airport. Apart from 'welcome', what topics might you talk about? Choose from the list or think of your own.

- comfortable flight?
- visited this country before?
- hungry or thirsty?
- the weather where they came from
- a brief history of your city
- what's going to happen in the next hour or so
- people and places in the visitor's country that you know

For each one you choose, what would your first sentence be?

2 You are at a reception for an international tourism fair in your city. Work in two groups.

Group A: Meeters and greeters

You are working at the reception. Your job is to welcome each of the guests and begin a short conversation. You may want to offer something or introduce the guest to another person.

NOTES

Make sure that you treat each guest with the appropriate level of respect and formality.

Two of the guests should be people that you already know.

None of the guests should be left on their own.

You should meet and greet as many different guests as possible.

Group B: Guests

Write your name and job / position on a badge / label. Choose from this list or think of your own.

- a local hotel manager
- a local tour operator
- a local travel agent
- a tour guide
- the mayor of the city (a VIP)
- an invited guest from another country
- the driver who brought the mayor

When you have finished, change roles and repeat the activity.

Vocabulary

Car hire

Look at the online booking form for car hire at Cape Town airport.

1 Find words, phrases, or abbreviations that mean

1 four doors with air-conditioning
2 automatic gears
3 move to a better service
4 insurance cover if you damage the hire car
5 insurance cover if you injure somebody or damage somebody's car
6 the glass at the front of a car
7 somewhere to put extra luggage on top of the car
8 an extra charge
9 the place where the petrol goes
10 money given as first part of a payment.

2 Find words which are the opposite of

1 automatic (for describing gears)
2 pick up
3 empty
4 maximum.

Car image	Capacity	Description Auto / Manual	Phone price	Online price	Booking
	x2 x2 / x1 x1	Economy 2dr Manual No air-con ❄	£202.00	£138.00 (€199.00)	BOOK NOW
	x2 x2 / x1 x1	Economy 4dr Manual No air-con ❄	£206.00	£141.00 (€203.00)	BOOK NOW
	x2 x2 / x1 x1	Economy 4dr / a/c Manual Air-con fitted ❄	£225.00	£153.00 (€220.00)	BOOK NOW
	x2 x3 / x1 x2	Compact 4dr / auto a/c Auto Air-con fitted ❄	£374.00	£252.00 (€363.00)	BOOK NOW

Your booking

Customer name: [Jacobson Mr]
Destination: [South Africa]
Pick-up location: [Cape Town Airport]
Drop-off location: ....
From: [11 August] To: ....
No. of days: ....
Age of driver: ....
Car selected: ....

Upgrade your car now to

☐ 5-seater 4 dr a/c for only £3 extra per day

Pre-bookable insurance options

☐ collision damage waiver
☐ third-party liability
☐ holiday auto damage excess waiver
☐ cancellation protection
☐ windscreen replacement cover

Extras payable locally at time of pick-up

☐ additional driver
☐ baby seat 0–1 years
☐ baby seat 1–3 years
☐ child seat 3 years +
☐ roof-rack

IMPORTANT INFORMATION

Minimum driver's age is 21. Drivers 18–20 will be subject to a surcharge of R100 per driver.
Your car will be supplied with a full tank of fuel and must be returned full.
You will be required to leave a deposit of R1,000. If the car is damaged, you may be charged an excess of between R980 and R4,900 depending on the size of the car (unless you purchase the 'holiday auto damage excess waiver').

Credit card payments must be in the name of the lead driver.
I confirm that I have read and understood the important information above and the car rentals terms and conditions section. ☐

You could drive a car around the world 4 times with the amount of fuel in a jumbo jet.

Listening

Car hire dialogue

1 🎧 Listen to someone picking up a car from the car hire desk at Cape Town airport. Complete the online booking form on p.8.

2 🎧 Listen again. Complete the questions used by the assistant for each of the prompts from a training guide.

1	Offer help Can _____?
2	Find out name What _____?
3	Online booking? Was _____?
4	Offer upgrade Would _____?
5	Check drop-off You're going to drop it off in ten days' time? Is _____?
6	Ask age Can you _____?
7	Offer additional insurance Do you _____?
8	Check / offer extras Do you _____?
9	Ask age of child How old _____?
10	Anything else? Is there _____?
11	Get signature Could you _____?
12	Ask method of payment How will _____?

3 Use the questions to practise the dialogue with a partner.

Pronunciation

1 Look at the names of different makes of car. How would you pronounce them in your language?

Make of car	Pronunciation
1 Chrysler	a /fɔːd/
2 Citroën	b /tɔɪˈjəʊtə/
3 Ford	c /ˈəʊpl/
4 Hyundai	d /ˈkraɪzlə/
5 Mercedes	e /məˈseɪdiːz/
6 Opel	f /ˈsɪtrən/
7 Renault	g /ˈhɪjʊndaɪ/
8 Toyota	h /ˈrenəʊ/

2 Match the names with their phonetic transcriptions.

3 🎧 Listen to the names. Compare the English pronunciation with the pronunciation in your own language. Pay attention to
1 which syllable the main stress is on
2 which consonant sounds are different
3 which vowel sounds are different.

4 Practise the English pronunciation of the different makes of car.

Speaking

Car hire at an airport

Work in pairs. Student A, you are the customer. Choose a car from the form on p.8 and invent booking details as you wish. Student B, you are the car hire agent.

Role-play the conversation, following these stages.
- Greeting
- Ask name
- Make special offer
- Check booking details
- Check insurance options
- Check extras
- Ask for payment
- Check for any other requests
- Explain collection arrangements
- Say goodbye

Now change roles.

What is it?

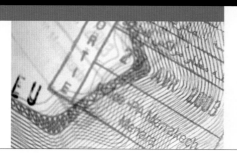

Vocabulary

Arriving and moving on

1 Look at the list of arrival places. Where do you find them?

EXAMPLES
at an airport, at a seaport, at a land border

1 domestic / international terminal
2 terminus
3 arrivals lounge
4 Customs
5 border control
6 immigration
7 harbour
8 meeting point

2 What happens at each place?

3 Match a word in A with a word in B. There may be more than one possibility.

A	B
1 accommodation	a booking service
2 car	b bus
3 city	c centre
4 connecting	d desk
5 information	e flight
6 rush	f hour
7 scheduled	g lounge
8 shuttle	h rank
9 taxi	i rental
10 transfer	j service
11 transit	

4 Complete the arrival information sheet using words from **3**.

If you have a _____¹ flight, please go to the _____² lounge.

There is a _____³ bus between the airport and the city centre. This scheduled _____⁴ takes approximately 30 minutes (45 minutes in the _____ _____⁵). Alternatively, you can go to the _____⁶ rank.

If you have pre-booked the transfer _____⁷, please go to the information _____⁸ to meet your driver.

If you have pre-booked a hire car, please go to the _____ _____⁹ desks.

Reading

Cape Town arrival information

1 In pairs, read these questions. Which of the words from *Vocabulary* do you think will appear in the answers?

1 How long will it take to drive from the airport to the city centre?
2 What transport services are available from the airport to the city centre?
3 Where can you find a taxi?
4 How much will a taxi cost?
5 Where do the intercity buses and mainline trains terminate?
6 Where can tourists find information?

2 Read the text and answer the questions in **1**.

3 Look at the text again. Find examples of sentences that include the following words.

there is / there are	operate(s)
you'll need	terminate(s)
you'll find	best place
if	everything you need
	must

4 For each sentence you found, write a different sentence.

EXAMPLE
(from the text) **There's a** scheduled service to the main train terminus.
(different sentence) **There's a** minibus service to the city.

Find out

What are the nearest international points of arrival to the place where you are studying? Research the different points – by air, land, and sea (if appropriate) – and find out as much about them as possible.

Writing

Arrival information

Write an arrival information sheet for your city or region. If appropriate, include sections on

- general arrival information
- airport to city / town centre
- intercity buses and trains
- other arrival points
- car hire
- information.

Checklist

Assess your progress in this unit. Tick (✓) the statements which are true.

- [ ] I can use different expressions for welcoming
- [ ] I can greet and make introductions
- [ ] I can carry out a car hire dialogue
- [ ] I can write about arrival information

Key words

Greetings
handshake
hospitality
welcome

Arrival and transport
arrivals lounge
border control
door-to-door
hub
rush hour
taxi rank
transit lounge

Car hire
automatic (gears)
CDW – collision damage waiver
drop-off
excess
manual (gears)
pick-up
pre-book
roof-rack
(fuel) tank
third-party liability
upgrade
windscreen

Next stop

1 What can you remember about the first time you stayed in a hotel? Tell your partner.

2 Do you like staying in hotels? Why (not)?

3 How do you think people who travel a lot feel about hotels?

Arriving in Cape Town

Airport

Cape Town International Airport (flight information, tel: 934 0407) is on the Cape Flats, 22 km and half an hour's drive (longer during rush hour) from the city centre.

Intercape operates two shuttle buses from the airport: there's a scheduled service to the main train terminus, running on the half hour and costing R30. From their office in the international terminal they operate a door-to-door transfer service which goes to anywhere on the Peninsula.

A cheaper door-to-door option is the 24-hour Backpackers Airport Shuttle, a minibus that takes passengers from the airport to anywhere in the city centre. The service operates in response to demand, which means you'll either need to pre-book or wait up to 45 minutes for them to get to the airport.

If you want to travel by car, there are taxi ranks outside the terminals (about R100 to the city centre). Please note that taxis must display the driver's name and a clearly visible meter. Inside the terminals you'll find the desks of the major car rental firms. There are no trains from the airport.

Intercity buses and trains

Greyhound, *Intercape*, and *Translux* intercity buses, and mainline trains from other provinces, all terminate in the centre of town around the interlinked central complex that includes the railway station and the Golden Acre shopping mall. Everything you need for your next move is within two or three blocks of here.

Information

The best place for information is the Cape Town Tourist Information Office, on the corner of Burg and Castle Sts.

2 A place to stay

Take off

1 Match the options in the questionnaire with the pictures.

2 Which two options would you choose? Why?

3 Which option has no picture?

4 What do you think this option means?

Questionnaire
Users' perceptions of hotels

What's a hotel for you? Choose one or two of the options below.

a A bed for the night ☐

b A place to hide away ☐

c Home from home ☐

d The office when away from the office ☐

e A bit of luxury once in a while ☐

f A place where you can let your hair down ☐

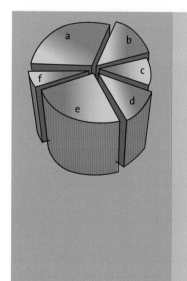

Reading
Client perceptions of hotels

1 Work in pairs.

1 The questionnaire in *Take off* was given to the guests of a major hotel company. Why do you think the company did the survey?

2 Who do you think the company sent the results to?
   a the company's hotel managers
   b their hotel staff
   c the staff at the local hotel training school

Read the start of the memo and see if you were right.

2 Now read the rest of the memo and answer the questions.

1 Which of the results do you find most surprising?

2 Why is it difficult to define what 'luxury' means to individual guests?

3 There are many ways a hotel can make itself a 'home'. Can you think of three?

4 What can a hotel do to be seen as a real 'office away from the office'?

5 Can you think of examples of film stars or pop stars 'letting their hair down'?

3 Which is most important for you when you travel away from home – feeling comfortable, feeling secure, or letting your hair down?

Dear Colleagues

Please study the enclosed results of our recent survey on client perceptions. These should then be commented on in your next staff training session.

Option A   32.8%

No surprise here – travel is tiring, and the average human body needs seven to eight hours' sleep a day. In this respect, the hotel responds to a basic, physiological need, and so above all else, we must provide a comfortable bed in a quiet room.

Option B   8.6%

Everyone needs to feel safe, so our hotels clearly have to generate a feeling of security. We can do this in simple ways: all rooms should have a solid door and lock; the reception area should always offer a sense of order; staff should never run or appear stressed, etc.

Option C   7.1%

The need to feel at home is equally important for frequent and less frequent travellers. However, while frequent travellers feel this way because they are not at home often enough, less frequent travellers appreciate the 'home from home' touch in a hotel precisely because of the strangeness of their new surroundings. Two obvious ways of making the hotel feel like home are a genuine smile from all staff that guests meet, and the use of the guest's name whenever possible. Please brainstorm others in the training session.

Option D   17.3%

Business travellers also have professional needs. In general, we probably need to improve what we offer here. An internet connection in a corner of the lobby is no longer enough.

Option E   31.4%

This should not come as a surprise. Our self-esteem is important to our overall health. The 'feel-good' factor of staying in hotels, then, is something that we need to keep in mind constantly as service providers. Please note, however, that exactly what each guest means by 'luxury' is not so easy to identify.

Option F   2.8%

This may be a surprise. We have too often assumed that for people away from home and on their own, a hotel would seem to be a great chance to do all those things they wouldn't normally dare to do. No colleagues, no friends, no family, etc! This turns out not to be so.

Find out

1   Use the questionnaire from *Take off*, and survey your family and friends about how they see hotels. Translate the questions if necessary. Interview ten people and invite them to comment on their choices.

2   Combine the results of the whole class.

3   With a partner, work out the percentages for each option and then produce a chart.

4   Use the comments from the interviews to illustrate your chart.

Customer care

Welcoming guests

Eight simple rules for welcoming guests
- Smile when you greet the customer
- Listen to what the customer is saying
- Make eye contact, but don't stare
- Make sure you look interested
- Address the customer by name
- Don't interrupt the customer
- Keep a reasonable distance from the customer, not too close and not too far
- Always thank the customer when appropriate

In groups of three, practise welcoming each other to your class 'hotel'. Take turns to be

A   the receptionist – ask some simple questions, e.g. about the journey

B   the guest – get the information you want

C   the monitor – watch the receptionist and see how many of the 'eight simple rules' he or she follows.

Key cards greatly increase security in today's hotels. They are re-programmed for each new guest, are cheaper to produce and replace than conventional keys, and can also be used for access to other hotel facilities such as the gym, or even the lifts.

Vocabulary

New arrivals

1 Match the terms in A with the definitions in B.

A		B	
1	to allocate	a	a plastic card with a magnetic strip for opening a door
2	identification	b	a paper document to show that a guest has already paid for a room
3	a guest history	c	the level of importance a guest has for a hotel
4	a key card	d	to give a guest a specific room
5	preferences	e	a card showing details of a guest's stay in a hotel
6	room rack	f	an important guest – either a regular (VIP 2) or a special guest (VIP 1)
7	a registration card	g	to pass a credit card through a terminal to register the card details
8	a walk-in	h	the computer screen or the board that shows which rooms are free
9	guest status	i	a computer file that shows details of a client's previous stays in a hotel
10	to swipe	j	e.g. smoking or non-smoking room, inside or outside room, near the lift, etc.
11	a VIP	k	e.g. a driving licence, a passport, an ID card, etc.
12	a voucher	l	a chance guest – someone who arrives without a room reservation

2 Complete the flow chart for the registration of a new arrival using words from A.

FAIRMONT HOTEL DURBAN

FRONT OFFICE PROCEDURES	
Process: Check-in & Check-out	Code: Chk. 01
Subprocess: Check-in	Revision: 1
	Date: 21/04/20–

Procedure 1 – individual arrivals with reservation

Greet guest
↓
Check reservation details on computer
↓
Ask for some form of _____ [1]
↓
Check guest _____ [2] for status and preferences
No history? → Subroutine 1
↓
Check _____ [3] and _____ [4] suitable room
↓
Check car parking needs
↓
Complete registration card
↓
_____ [5] credit card (or request agency _____ [6] if appropriate → Subroutine 2)
↓
Ask client to sign _____ [7]. Keep hotel section.
↓
Hand client registration card and _____ [8]
↓
Give room number and indicate location of lifts, restaurant, etc.
↓
Give details of breakfast service
↓
Welcome guest

Front office Why is it called the front office? Because working in the front office makes you the first and last person the guest sees in the hotel. You will be responsible for the all-important first impressions that the guest receives. You can't get much more 'up front' than that!

Listening

Registration procedures

1 Listen and identify the three types of guests.

Type of guest	Dialogue
1 New guest with a reservation	
2 Regular guest (VIP 2)	
3 Chance guest	

2 Listen to each arrival again. How were you able to tell which was which?

3 Listen to the whole of dialogue c and complete these sentences.

1 Good evening, sir. _____ can I _____ you?

2 Could I just _____ some _____, please, Mr Scott?

3 And will you be _____ the _____?

4 Will you be _____ by _____ card?

5 Could I just _____ your card a _____, please, to _____ it?

6 And if you could _____ _____ here on the registration card?

7 And _____ is your _____ card.

Pronunciation

1 Look at this phrase.

How can I **help** you?

The word in **bold** is the key word in the phrase. We need to be sure the client hears this word. Practise doing this by saying the key word first. Then add other words, like this:

1 … **help**?   3 … can I **help** you?

2 … **help** you?   4 How can I **help** you?

2 Listen and do the same with the other phrases in *Listening* **3** until you are fluent with all of them.

Speaking

Registering new arrivals

1 Guests with a reservation.

```
                    C H E C K - I N
Reservation number: HSMO-011106
Rm type: SB                Terms: B&B
No. rms: 1                 Rate:  120
-----------------------------------------------
Arrive: 21.04.08           ETA:   18.00
Nights: 4
Depart: 25.04.08           Pre-asig. rm(s): 408
-----------------------------------------------
Name:     Moyer            Initials: A.R.  VIP: --
Address:  A. Nováka, 78    Tel:   +420 1433 9967
          880 66 Brno      Email: novakaa@ph.uni.cz
Nationality: Czech         ID:    --
Guest 2: --
Guest 3: --               Garage: --
-----------------------------------------------
Deposit: NO          Due: --    Received: --
Reservation by: Michel        Payment: Amer. Exp.
Voucher/Credit card no.:    5672 3410 82382 4078
-----------------------------------------------
Comments: Non-smoking, lower floors
-----------------------------------------------
  [F2-Guest history] [F7-print] [F8-Arrivals]
```

1 Work in pairs. Student A, you are the receptionist. Look at the information on the computer screen. Check with the guest that all the details are correct. If they are, issue the key card and tell the guest which room and floor they are staying on. Student B, you are the guest.

2 Now change roles and repeat the activity.

2 Guests without a reservation.

Student A, you are the guest. Go to p.108. Student B, you are the receptionist. Go to p.116. Use the computer screen to help you to register your guest.

3 Make up your own data. You can be a guest with or without a reservation. You can be a regular guest (VIP 2) or a very important guest (VIP 1). Act out your conversation.

I recruit personalities. I can teach someone how to run a hotel but I can't give them a personality. If they're computer literate, then we can teach them to use the hotel computer package they need to work reception. But if there's a guest in the lift and a member of staff too, they've got to have personality. They can't just ignore the guest.

Georgiy Kulyk
Hotel Mayakovsky, Kiev

● Language spot
Where things are

1 Look at the hotel plan.

1 Find the breakfast room, the Cordon Bleu restaurant, and the ground floor lifts.

2 Now find the hairdresser's, the gift shop, and Meeting room 1. Where are they?

3 🎧 Listen to the receptionist and check your answers.

> The breakfast room is **in the basement.**

> The lifts are **over there next to** the concierge's desk.

> The restaurant is here **on the ground floor.**

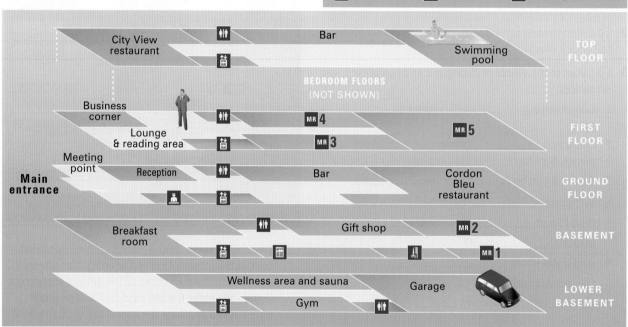

2 You are the receptionist. How would you answer these guests?

1 Excuse me, where's the garage?
2 Excuse me, do you have a gym?
3 Excuse me, are there toilets near the wellness area?
4 Excuse me, is there a business corner in the hotel?
5 Hi, have you got a swimming pool?

3 Work in pairs. Student A, you are the guest. Choose six places in the hotel. Ask where the places are. Student B, you are the receptionist. Answer Student A's questions.

Now change roles.

>> Go to **Grammar reference** p.118

Speaking
Tell me where

1 Think about the building you study in. Think of five places a visiting student might need to find. Be the student and ask your partner where they are.

2 Now change roles and answer your partner's questions.

3 Think about where you live. How many rooms are there, which rooms are they, and where are they?

4 Tell your partner about where you live. Your partner has to draw a floor plan as he / she listens. When you have finished, check the plan.

The three-star Ostfriesland Hotel in Norden, Germany, has the world's most unusual tariff system for rooms. Guests pay according to how much they weigh at a rate of €0.50 per kilogram. Somebody weighing 53 kg will pay just €26.50 a night, including breakfast.

Reading

Hotel services

1 Look quickly through the hotel leaflet below. When would you expect to be given this leaflet?

1. on arrival
2. on leaving the hotel
3. on asking about a particular hotel service

2 Read the leaflet again and write T (true) or F (false).

1. The hotel can make photocopies for business guests, but charges for the service.
2. The hotel has car parking for only a few cars, so it is best to reserve a parking space before you arrive.
3. The hotel accepts all disabled guests.
4. You can check out of the hotel by yourself using the TV in your room.
5. You are not allowed to take food to your room.
6. You can leave a mobile phone charging its batteries in your room while you go out for a meal.

3 Find all the prepositions of place in the texts.

4 Work in groups. What hotel services can you think of for the letters of the alphabet that did not appear in the leaflet?

Writing

Hotel information

1 Work in groups of four or five. Make a list of all the services a hotel can offer in the following areas.

- eating and drinking
- recreation and relaxation
- business services
- room service and facilities
- local transport and other services

2 Take responsibility for one of the five areas. Write the texts for the information for your services.

3 Swap texts. Check one of your partner's texts for mistakes. Check especially the prepositions of place.

4 Together prepare a Services Directory with all of your descriptions.

Business services

Fax and photocopying services are available at Reception. Prices on request. There is a modem socket in each room for internet connections. Any calls that are made will be charged to your account.

Car parking

There are a limited number of spaces at the hotel available on a first come, first parked basis. All vehicles parked in the car park are parked at the owner's risk. The hotel accepts no responsibility for any loss or damage caused to cars parked in the car park.

Disabled facilities

The hotel has a limited number of bedrooms suitable for the partially disabled.

Express checkout

This facility is available via your TV. Switch your TV on, press INFO on your remote control, then choose option 6 to view your account, and option 7 to check out of your room.

Food

A wide variety of Takeaway Menus are available at Reception. Takeaways can be enjoyed in the Bar on the ground floor, the Breakfast Room on the first floor, or in the comfort of your bedroom.

Green policy

The hotel has adopted some policies in the interest of the environment:
Only towels left in the bath will be changed.

To conserve energy, the electricity supply to your room is controlled by the box on the wall near the door. To switch on the power, place your key card in the slot in the top of the box when you enter the room. Remove the key card when you leave, and the electricity will be switched off automatically.

Heating

The hotel has heating on from October to April.

Listening

The staff structure of hotels

1 Look at these hotel staff titles. Say if the people would work in

1   the front office
2   housekeeping
3   food and beverages.

kitchen assistant
chambermaid
concierge
front office manager
head chef
head waiter
housekeeper
porter
receptionist

2 🎧 Roberta is the General Manager of the Hotel Concordia in Milan. Listen to her talking about the staff structure of the hotel and complete the diagram.

3 🎧 Listen again and answer the questions.

1   What does the food and beverages department cover?
2   How many housekeepers does Carlotta have in the high season?
3   Why does Roberta prefer the term *housekeeper* over *chambermaid*?
4   What does Silvio do?

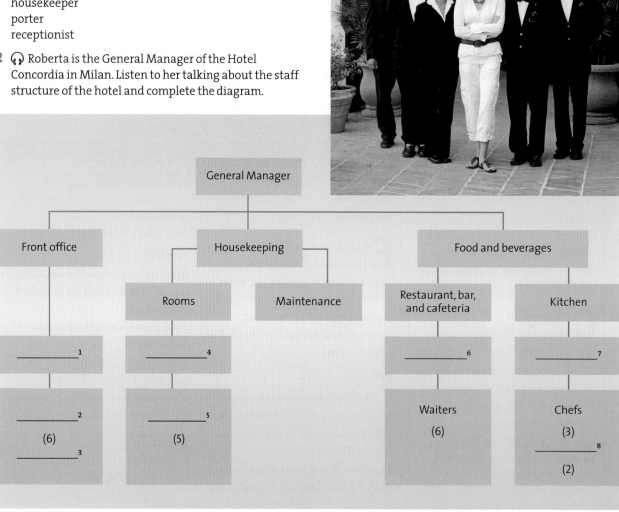

It's my job

Grzegorz Rosinski

Grzegorz works as a concierge in a hotel in Krakow, Poland. He says there is never a dull moment in his job, which brings him into direct contact with guests every day. What sorts of skills do you need to be a concierge? What sorts of things do guests ask? What have hot-air balloons got to do with Grzegorz's work? Read on and find out.

Can you tell me three things you need to be able to do your job well?

You need to be a bit of a psychologist to understand your guests. That's a key part of good customer services. You need English to be able to speak to international guests. And you need good communication skills.

How about three things you do most often?
1 Make dining reservations and obtain tickets for events
2 Provide information about local facilities and services such as shopping, dining, nightlife, and so on
3 Make travel arrangements

What do guests ask you for most often?
What is there to do in the city? Can you recommend a nice restaurant for us? What is the local food? Where are we on the map? How do I get to the airport?

What's the thing you most like doing?
Planning special events, discos, parties, and celebrations. It includes booking performers and celebrities, and I get to meet them. They're often really nice.

What's the most unusual request you've ever had?
That's easy! We had a couple on their honeymoon and they wanted to see the city from a hot-air balloon. It was easy to find a balloonist, but we couldn't get permission to fly free over the city. In the end the balloon was launched in a park behind the hotel, but tied to the ground all the time.

Checklist

Assess your progress in this unit. Tick (✓) the statements which are true.

- [ ] I can understand reports describing guests' perceptions of hotels
- [ ] I can register different types of arriving guests
- [ ] I can tell guests where different hotel facilities are in the building
- [ ] I can give accurate information about hotel services and facilities
- [ ] I can understand people talking about hotel staffing

Key words

Nouns	Verbs
chambermaid	allocate
chance guest	charge
concierge	register
food and beverages	swipe
front office	
guest history	
guest status	
housekeeper	
identification	
key card	
kitchen assistant	
maintenance	
registration card	
room rack	
survey	
VIP	
voucher	
walk-in	

Next stop

1 Have you ever had to find out information on tourist attractions and services (e.g. opening times, entrance costs), or travel facilities or times?

2 Where do you obtain this information?

3 What do you think is the best way to get this information?

4 Do you have any examples of good or bad information service?

3 Tourist information services

Take off

1 How many different ways of providing information to tourists can you think of? Use the photos to help you.

EXAMPLE
printed brochures and leaflets

2 What types of encounters with the public do they involve?

EXAMPLE
face-to-face (at a Tourist Information Centre)

3 What types of questions do the public ask?

EXAMPLE
Directions (How can I get to the castle?)

Vocabulary

Information types

1 Which of the headings (a–i) from a tourist information website will give information on

1	accommodation?	a	What's on
2	events?	b	Walks and tours
3	attractions?	c	Book-a-bed-ahead
4	children's activities?	d	This month's featured
5	transport?		events
6	guided tours?	e	Places to visit
7	emergencies?	f	Emergency health care
		g	Places to stay
		h	Family fun
		i	Getting about

2 Which of these words do you associate with

1 a Tourist Information Centre?
2 a website?
3 other information sources?

a	click	i	FAQs
b	display rack	j	helpline
c	recorded information	k	listings
d	leaflet	l	maps
e	home page	m	touch screen
f	reception	n	interactive
g	call centre	o	customer care
h	search		

In this unit
● Tourist Information Centres
● giving directions
● making recommendations

Reading

Tourist Information Centres

Read the article.

1 How many ways of presenting information are mentioned?
2 What services are mentioned?
3 What skills are important if you work in a TIC?
4 Can a website provide the same services as a TIC?
5 What are the relative advantages and disadvantages of TICs and websites as sources of information for tourists and visitors?

Inside tourism: information

Tourist information comes in a variety of forms, but the two most important are probably Tourist Information Centres (TICs) and websites.

TICs are found in city centres, major resorts, and transport termini. Tourist information offices, which may be smaller than TICs, are also found in smaller towns and rural areas. Inside the TIC there will be displays of leaflets and brochures on local attractions, entertainment venues and events, transport information such as timetables and schedules, and listings of accommodation providers. Many TICs have touch-screen facilities and interactive information displays, as well as trained staff.

Staff will be expected to provide information on a range of areas – such as which restaurant provides a high chair for a baby, the best place for a scenic walk or drive, how to get to local sights, and where the nearest toilets are. Some TICs will have an accommodation booking service, including booking accommodation at the next destination for tourists who are travelling around the region. They may also be able to reserve theatre tickets, arrange car rental, book an excursion or a guide, change currency, and even make an emergency dental appointment.

To work in a TIC, a pleasant and helpful personality is essential. You should have a good telephone manner, be able to work with computers, and have good written skills. Knowledge of a foreign language is also useful.

Customer care

Assessing customer types

Customers come in all shapes and sizes. Working in a Tourist Information Centre, you will meet people with very different characteristics and ways of behaving.

Here are some customer types. Do you recognize any of the types from people you know or have dealt with?

● **The questioner:** asks lots and lots of questions even though they don't really need to know
● **Straight to the point:** wants a clear simple answer to their query, and nothing extra
● **Empty head:** not sure what they want to know, but feel they ought to ask something
● **The shy one:** wants help but won't ask for it
● **Know-it-all:** wants to tell you how much *they* know
● **The sponge:** fascinated by everything you have to say and absorbs all the information

How would you deal with these customer types? Would you treat them all the same?

Find out

1 Research information services in your city or region, for example

● Tourist Information Centres
● websites
● guidebooks.

2 Collect as many examples of tourist information material as possible, including (if possible) English-language information material. Make sure you have at least one street map. This material will be useful in some of the later activities in this unit.

Listening

Tourist information

1 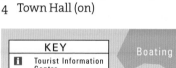 Listen to these extracts from different sources of tourist information. Decide if the information is

  a a recorded information line
  b given face-to-face
  c from a phone helpline.

2 Listen again. What information is the enquirer asking about? Choose from this list.

	1	2	3	4	5
a sights to visit					
b visas					
c train availability					
d theatre tickets					
e art galleries					
f booking accommodation					
g currency exchange					
h guided excursions					
i child-friendly restaurants					
j local maps					

3 Read the listening script on p.129 to check.

4 Note down the expressions that the tourism employees use to offer help.

Speaking

Giving information

1 Work in pairs. For each of the nine website headings a–i in *Vocabulary 1* on p.20, think of a piece of information for your city or region.

2 Compare your information with another pair.

3 Take turns to role-play dialogues in the TIC asking for and giving information on the different headings.

Listening

How do I get to . . . ?

Look at the map of Southwold, a seaside resort in England.

1 Describe the location of the following places, using the preposition in brackets.

  1 TIC (next to)
  2 disabled toilets (opposite)
  3 disabled toilets (between)
  4 Town Hall (on)
  5 Sailors' Reading Room (at the end of)
  6 school (near)

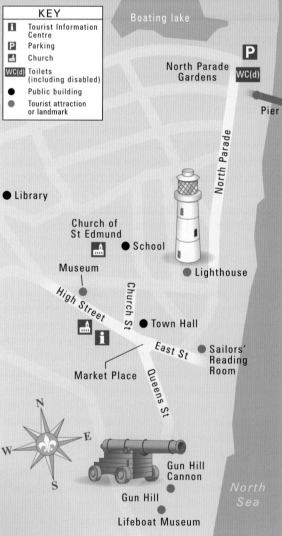

KEY

🅸	Tourist Information Centre
🅿	Parking
⛪	Church
WC(d)	Toilets (including disabled)
●	Public building
●	Tourist attraction or landmark

Where do you find them?

2 🎧 Listen to a tourist information officer giving directions from the TIC. Follow the routes and identify the places he is describing.

3 🎧 Listen again and complete the directions.

a   When _____ ¹ of the Information Centre, turn right and _____ ² the High Street. Walk on through the Market Place _____ ³ a fork in the road. If you take the _____ ⁴ and go along Queen Street, _____ ⁵ some nice antique shops and a small art gallery and eventually _____ ⁶ a green hill. _____ ⁷ the hill _____ ⁸ the cannon and you're there.

b   The best way is to _____ ¹ Church Street – it's just _____ ² to the right; can you see it? If you turn right _____ ³ Church Street, _____ ⁴ a lovely little green and _____ ⁵ the lighthouse – you can't _____ ⁶ it. Just _____ ⁷ the lighthouse and then the seafront is just _____ ⁸ you. When you get to the seafront, _____ ⁹ and you can either _____ ¹⁰ the beach or the cliff. You'll see it in the distance sticking out to sea. It _____ ¹¹ any longer than fifteen minutes.

● Language spot

Giving directions and prepositions of movement

1 Which of the following are spoken by someone *giving* directions?
1   The best way to go is …
2   How do you get to … ?
3   Do you want the most direct route?
4   If you turn left here, …
5   I'm trying to get to the station.
6   What you need to do is …

2 Match the phrases in A with the places in B. There will often be more than one possibility.

A		B	
1	go along	a	the TIC
2	walk towards	b	the hill
3	come out of	c	the street
4	get to	d	a bus
5	walk on through	e	the city centre
6	turn right out of	f	the bar
7	turn right at	g	the park
8	reach	h	the fork in the road
9	take	i	the right-hand turn
10	go past	j	the market

3 Choose two of the pairings and try to link them using *if, when, until,* or *and*.

EXAMPLE
Go along the street <u>until</u> you come to the market.

4 In pairs, use the map of Southwold to give each other directions to different places.

5 Use some of the maps you collected in *Find out* to practise asking for and giving directions in your own city or region.

≫ Go to **Grammar reference** p.119

Top three annual European Amusement / Theme Park Admissions

1 Disneyland Paris = 12.0 million
2 Blackpool Pleasure Beach, UK = 6.0 million
3 Tivoli Gardens, Copenhagen = 3.9 million

Pronunciation

1 🎧 Listen to the phrases from *Language spot*. Notice how the words link together.

1 come‿out‿of
2 walk‿on
3 head‿up
4 turn right‿out‿of
5 turn left‿at

2 Consonant or vowel? Choose the right word and complete the rule about linking.

> When a word ends in a *consonant / vowel* and the next word begins with a *consonant / vowel*, we link the words together.

3 Practise saying these phrases, paying attention to the linking.

1 Walk along the street.
2 Turn left at the shops …
3 Come out of the market …
4 Go past a fork in the road …
5 Walk on past a bus stop …
6 Head along this street and up a small hill.
7 Turn right at the museum, then go left at a fork in the road.
8 Turn left out of the TIC, head up a hill, and go past a park.

Reading

Liverpool

1 What do you know about Liverpool? Use the pictures to help you. Do you know anything about the 'maritime, cultural, and architectural history', or the 'musical and sporting excellence'?

2 Which information category 1–5 do you associate with adjectives a–i?

1 nightlife	a active	f famous
2 sport	b dazzling	g luxurious
3 shopping	c designer	h trendy
4 accommodation	d diverse	i wild
5 theme parks	e exhilarating	

3 Read the extracts from Tourist Information leaflets and websites. Check your answers to **1** and **2**.

Liverpool, European Capital of Culture in 2008, is a vibrant modern city in the north-west of England with a rich maritime, cultural, and architectural history, and a reputation for musical and sporting excellence.

1   No trip to Liverpool is complete without a visit to either Anfield, home of the famous Liverpool Football Club, or Goodison Park, home of their rivals Everton.

2   Liverpool is arguably best known for The Beatles and you can find reminders of their unique legacy all over the city. The Cavern Club, where The Beatles gave their early performances, is well worth visiting. Don't leave Liverpool without visiting The Beatles Museum or the childhood home of Paul McCartney.

3 I n a city with such a wealth of musical achievement, you would expect a dazzling and diverse nightlife. And that's exactly what Liverpool offers. If you're looking for a good night out, then why not visit the waterfront Albert Dock complex where you can find bars, restaurants, and club venues, as well as the famous Tate Gallery Liverpool?

4 During the day, why not try some 'retail therapy'? Liverpool City Centre boasts some of the largest big name High Street stores in the country, and at Albert Dock you can find many trendy designer stores.

5 As you'd expect for a city of this size, there is a huge choice on offer. Whether you're after a luxurious four-poster bed in a modern international hotel or a bunk bed in a city centre hostel that's within walking distance of the bars and clubs after a wild night out, our Accommodation Booking Service can make a booking for you.

6 If you want to get out and about and be active, you could start at Pleasureland at Southport: it's exhilarating entertainment for all the family, and home of the Traumatizer roller coaster – a must for all thrill-seekers.

● Language spot

Recommending and promoting

1 Look back at the extracts in *Reading*.
1 Find three examples of sentences using *You can find* … .
2 Find examples of sentences starting with *if* and *whether*. Which of them is used when giving two options?
3 Find the word *must*. Is it used as a noun or a verb? What preposition follows it?

2 Find examples of these words and phrases and write out the recommendation expression in full.
1 without (× 2) 3 worth
2 why not 4 you could

Which ones use the gerund or noun (e.g. *visiting* or *a visit*), and which use the bare infinitive (e.g. ~~to~~ *visit*)?

3 Complete this description of Copenhagen.

_____ ¹ you're a lover of history or a lover of culture, Copenhagen can offer you a fabulous experience. You can _____ ² lots of examples of interesting architecture, and Rosenborg Castle, home of the crown jewels, is well _____ ³ visiting. A trip to Legoland is a _____ ⁴ for all families with young children. _____ ⁵ you're looking for a relaxing walk, _____ ⁶ not visit the Tivoli Gardens? Finally, don't _____ ⁷ Copenhagen_____ ⁸ visiting the harbour to see the Little Mermaid statue.

4 The expressions listed in **1** and **2** are mainly *written* ways of making recommendations. Look at the list of expressions below. Which ones
1 are mainly spoken forms?
2 are mainly written forms?
3 could equally be written or spoken?

a If I were you, I'd …
b One of the best experiences you can have is …
c I've got an idea: why don't you …
d I'd recommend –ing …
e There's no better place for _____ than …
f You might like to think about …
g Have you thought about …
h Your best option is …
i For a really memorable experience, you should …

5 Complete the *spoken* expressions for a visitor to your city or region. Use a different information topic each time (e.g. *accommodation, nightlife, shopping*). Make recommendations to your partner.

>> Go to **Grammar reference** p.119

branding (n) the use of a particular name, symbol, and design for a company's product so that people will recognize them

citizen (n) a person who is legally accepted as a member of a particular country

flea market (n) a market, often in a street, that sells old and used goods

innovative (adj) creating new things, ideas, or ways of doing something

off the beaten track in a place where people do not often go

Where in the world?

Read about the award-winning Copenhagen Tourist Information Centre.

1 What type of information does it give?

2 What is unusual about the way in which the information is presented?

3 Do you think a TIC like this would be good in your town or city?

Copenhagen Right Now

The Copenhagen Right Now tourist information office is very popular indeed. Last year, more than 400,000 tourists visited the redesigned centre just opposite the main entrance to Tivoli Gardens.

Now, the tourist information centre has been awarded the annual prize for best **branding** by VisitDenmark, the official Danish board of tourism.

The prize is a recognition of the **innovative** and highly user-centred design concept. The idea was to build a hub for the information that visitors truly want when visiting Copenhagen – information about what is happening right now.

This information is not traditionally found in travel guides or agencies. For instance, *Copenhagen Right Now* guides the visitor to interesting spots, local venues, and other locations **off the beaten track.**

Tourists can discover such things as: where do the locals go for a good cup of coffee, or how does one see Copenhagen in three hours ...

A collection of display cases takes relevant information such as posters, flyers, and the like from the city's fences, and is a reflection of what is happening in the city right now, from **flea markets** and hip hop concerts to ballets and operas.

A database of **citizens** of Copenhagen tells the visitors which shops, restaurants, bars, and parks the locals like and dislike, in order to let the visitor know what the ordinary Copenhagener finds cool and uncool.

Read more about Copenhagen Right Now at www.visitcopenhagen.dk or visit the centre at: 4A Vesterbrogade, Copenhagen V, Tel: +45 70 222 442.

Writing

Recommendations

Write a tourist information advice and recommendation sheet for your own area. You should include the following sections. Try to use all of the expressions from *Language spot*.

Tourist information in ...

A general description

Information on natural features

Places to visit (e.g. museums, historic buildings)

Nightlife and entertainment

Shopping

Accommodation

Other important information

Checklist

Assess your progress in this unit. Tick (✓) the statements which are true.

- [ ] I can understand and describe different ways of giving tourist information
- [ ] I can give directions in spoken and written forms
- [ ] I can make recommendations in spoken and written forms

Key words

Nouns
call centre
display rack
FAQs
helpline
home page
leaflet
lighthouse
listings
recorded information
seafront
statue
touch screen
tourist information centre (TIC)

Adjectives
child-friendly
dazzling
designer
disabled
exhilarating
interactive
maritime
trendy

Verb
click

Next stop

1 What does a holiday representative for a tour operator do?

2 Have you ever seen a tour operator's holiday rep at work meeting new arrivals at an airport or working with tourists in a hotel?

3 Have you ever been on a holiday where you were met by a holiday rep?

4 Holiday rep

Take off

1 Look at the pictures. Choose one that shows something you have done. Tell your partner about it.

2 Which picture is not about a type of holiday rep?

3 Match each of the three texts with a picture. Tell your partner the connection.

1 Two years ago I went to Crete with two of my friends. It was a brilliant holiday. The weather was perfect and I loved the way of life, so after speaking to one of the reps I decided not to go back to Britain. And now I'm a rep! And here comes my group – bound for the airport and home.

2 This is a job for people who really love the outdoors. We're out in all weathers – putting up and taking down tents, cleaning, organizing activities. Mostly the weather's fine, but if it's rainy, it's hard work. And if it's windy, it's almost impossible!

3 I trained as a teacher, but I didn't want to go straight into a full-time job. So I came out here for a season. I organize games and activities, sports sessions – anything to keep the kids busy! I love working with them. The teaching? Maybe next year!

In this unit
- types of holiday reps
- giving a welcome meeting talk
- advice and obligation
- holiday health
- tips on tipping

Listening

A rep for all seasons

1 Look at the types of rep. What do you think each one does?

1 Campsite courier	4 Club rep	7 Transfer rep
2 Chalet host	5 Family rep	
3 Children's rep	6 Ski rep	

2 🎧 Listen to four reps introducing themselves. Write which type of rep each person is under their name.

3 Look at the duties and responsibilities in the table.

1 Do you understand them all? Use your dictionary if necessary.

2 Guess which duties are true for Jason and Luke. Mark each one with a tick (✔).

3 🎧 Listen to Jason and Luke and check your answers.

4 Who seems happier – Jason or Luke? How can you tell?

5 Which of the two jobs would you prefer? Tell your partner why.

Speaking

A day in the life of ...

1 What do you think the duties are for the other two reps? Mark them with a cross (✗).

2 Compare your guesses with your partner's and explain your choices.

3 Work in pairs. Student A, go to p.110. Student B, go to p.112.

1 Study the job description. Order your responsibilities from the most to the least interesting in your opinion.

2 Introduce yourself to your partner and describe your job. Say where you work and what you do. Explain what you like and don't like about your job.

Duties and responsibilities \ Type of rep	1 Jason	2 Luke	3 Katerina	4 Anne Marie
a Accommodation, health and safety checks				
b Answering customers' queries / problems				
c Collecting and balancing foreign money				
d Conducting welcome meetings / selling excursions				
e Guiding excursions				
f Organizing entertainment, i.e. pool parties, bar crawls, party nights, etc.				
g Performing in cabarets which can be singing or games				
h Transferring holidaymakers to and from the airport				

What essential kit does a rep need?

Reading

Resort representative

1 Holiday reps work very hard. Read the job description and decide which aspects of their job

1 have to be done once with each group of holidaymakers
2 have to be done once a day
3 have to be done several times during a holiday
4 mean being available almost 24/7 (24 hours a day / 7 days a week).

2 Answer the questions.

1 'Representatives' work is seasonal'. What does *seasonal* mean here?
2 'Hours of work are variable'. What does *variable* mean here?

3 Work in small groups.

1 Make a list of skills and personal qualities that a holiday rep needs.
2 Which skills and qualities do you have? Tell your partners.

So you want to be a resort representative?

The work

Resort representatives are the first point of contact for holidaymakers at their destination. They represent the tour operator, and aim to ensure the success of the clients' holidays.

Representatives meet each party of holidaymakers on their arrival at the airport and accompany them by coach to their accommodation. Usually, they hold a welcome meeting soon after arrival to give the holidaymakers information about resort facilities and attractions.

Resort representatives arrange regular times to meet holidaymakers to make announcements and deal with enquiries and problems. They keep an information board, and often a folder of useful information, up-to-date. They may also arrange, book, and sometimes accompany excursions and sightseeing trips and arrange car or ski hire.

In addition to this they need to be available at almost any time to give advice, solve problems, and deal with emergencies such as loss of passports or money, illness, or difficulties with accommodation.

The completion of paperwork is an important aspect of the job. This involves keeping records and writing reports of complaints and incidents such as illness.

Hours and environment

Representatives' work is seasonal. Depending on the resort / country, holiday seasons may run from April onwards, October to January or January to April. Hours of work are variable. Representatives often work from early morning to late evening and at weekends and can be on call 24 hours a day.

A driving licence is usually needed, as representatives need to travel between hotels or other holiday accommodation and may be responsible for a wide area.

Skills and personal qualities

As a resort representative you should be self-confident, with a pleasant, cheerful, and outgoing nature

Listening

Welcome to paradise!

... a welcome meeting soon after arrival to give the holidaymakers information about resort facilities and attractions.

1 You are going to hear a talk about welcome meetings. Look at the points covered in the talk and put them in order.

a socialize briefly
b smile and welcome
c meet the resort manager
d describe tourist attractions
e describe hotel facilities
f describe excursions
g check paperwork
h check complimentary drinks
i answer any questions

2 🎧 Listen and check your answers.

3 🎧 Listen again. Answer the questions.

1 Who is giving the talk?
2 Who is listening?
3 When do the reps have to look for the resort manager?
4 How long should a welcome meeting last? Why?
5 What is important to sell excursions?
6 Why is it important to socialize?

Pronunciation

1 🎧 Listen to the words from the resort manager's talk. How is the final s pronounced? Tick (✓) the correct column.

	/s/	/z/	/ɪz/
1 arrangements			
2 arrivals			
3 changes			
4 customers			
5 drinks			
6 excursions			
7 facilities			
8 notes			
9 places			

2 How is the final s pronounced in these words?

1 basics
2 beaches
3 bikes
4 buses
5 documents
6 fares
7 hours
8 lifts
9 meals
10 telephones
11 timetables
12 tours

3 Practise saying the words, paying attention to the final s.

Speaking

A welcoming talk

1 Work in pairs. You are going to give a welcome meeting talk.

1 Read the notes on the Sunseeker Holidays clipboard. Use your dictionary if necessary.

2 Look at the first eight points. Use the rep's notes and decide what you would say for each.

3 Divide the eight points up. Student A, prepare and practise four points. Student B, prepare and practise the other four.

4 Together, give your talk to another pair, who will mark you.

Sunseeker Holidays
Welcome meeting key points

Introduce yourself and partner. Introduce resort manager
Give contact telephones 954 667 8952 / 664 899 562

Hotel basics
- meals – breakfast 07.30–10.00h / lunch 12.30–15.00h / supper 19.30–22.00h
- Sunseekers announcements board – usually reception area opposite lifts
- problems with accommodation – 1st hotel reception. Not happy? Contact reps

Sunbathing
- how long – 20 mins. max first few days
- sunscreens – minimum factor 15 – more for nose, ears, etc.

Local transport
- taxis – fares = metre & tipping = round up / 5%
- local buses – timetables & fares – hotel announcements board
- bike, moped, & car hire – contact reps

Local attractions
- best beaches
- inland tours
- excursions
- the old town
- local food, etc.

Any questions

2 Watch your two colleagues give their welcome talk. Mark them from 1 (poor) to 5 (excellent) on

a clarity
b speed
c fluency
d enthusiasm
e coordination.

burn-out (*n*) the state of being extremely tired or ill, either physically or mentally, because you have worked too hard

flirt (*v*) to behave towards sb as if you find them sexually attractive, without seriously wanting to have a relationship with them

gossip (*n*) informal talk or stories about other people's private lives, that may be unkind or not true

It's my job

Ameli Destivelle

Ameli works in Teigne in the French Alps. Here she gives us her advice for surviving your first season as a ski rep. Check you understand the headings for each tip. What do you think Ameli is going to say about each heading? Read on and find out.

Tips for surviving the season ...

Flirting   A key part of any ski season. Workers should flirt with each other a lot. But don't forget: 'the flirting stops when you start taking it seriously.'

Gossip   Remember that gossip is an essential part of the ski rep's world. Don't expect to have a 'private' life. You may imagine it's just the two of you in on your little 'secret', but do you really know who saw you leave together last night?

Burn-out   At the start of the season, you might want to ski all day and party all night. Doing this on holiday is hard enough, but try doing it when you've got to get up at 7.00 a.m. six days a week. Burn-out, often combined with flu,

usually hits after New Year. Avoid this by pacing yourself – get an early night at least twice a week.

Day off   There's only one a week, so most staff use it wisely for either a big ski day or a big sleep day. The ski-hungry should check the forecast before getting drunk – this is your one chance to be first on the snow each week and you don't want to wake up at 11.00 a.m. to find you've missed the best powder day of the season.

Changeover day   There's no real way to prepare you for this. If you're working for a tour operator, there's no doubt this is the worst day of the week. For reps, a twenty-hour day is not uncommon: flight delays, lost luggage, traffic jams, and lost ski-pass photos will all feature.

● Language spot

Advice and obligation

Ameli's advice is for new ski reps. But what advice should holidaymakers get?

1 Complete the sentences using *avoid, don't, have to, mustn't,* or *should.*

   1 In hot weather, you _____ drink a lot of water and keep the sun off your head.

   2 _____ lying in the sun too long during the first few days of your holiday.

   3 _____ go swimming after eating a heavy meal or drinking alcohol.

   4 You _____ jump or dive into the hotel swimming pools.

   5 You _____ put sunscreen on again after you have been swimming.

   6 You _____ tell the rep and the hotel staff if you are allergic to anything.

   7 In less developed regions, _____ eating uncooked dairy products, vegetables, and salads.

2 Which of the expressions give advice and which describe an obligation?

3 Now write advice about safety and security for visitors.

1 _____ convert traveller's cheques on a daily basis.

2 _____ carry more cash than you need.

3 _____ come out of the sea if the lifeguards tell you to.

4 _____ know where the nearest fire exit is in your hotel.

5 _____ open the door of your room to a person you don't know.

6 _____ carry a wallet in the back pocket of your trousers or jeans.

7 _____ swim in the sea when the red flags are flying.

8 _____ use credit cards for larger purchases.

9 _____ walking down dark streets late at night.

>> Go to **Grammar reference** p.120

Vocabulary

Holiday health

1 Look at the health problems in B. How many do you recognize?

2 Can you add any more expressions?

3 Match expressions in A with continuations from B.

A	B
1 I'm …	a a rash
2 I've got …	b a sore throat
3 I feel …	c allergic to …
4 It's …	d an upset stomach
	e bruised
	f diabetic
	g diarrhoea
	h dizzy
	i red
	j sick
	k sunburn
	l sunburnt
	m swollen
	n toothache
	o unwell

4 Which are the most common problems for tourists

1 at a beach resort?
2 travelling in a tropical climate?
3 doing adventure tourism?

Customer care

Have you got the right attitude?

Every member of overseas staff is a representative of the organization and should always have a positive attitude to customers, acting in a professional manner at all times. There are certain rules you must respect.

Decide which of these rules are in the 'always' section, and which are in the 'never' section.

1 Be loyal to the organization.

2 Respect the buildings and equipment where you work.

3 Criticize the organization to, or in front of, customers.

4 Be friendly and courteous with both colleagues and customers.

5 Argue or swear in front of customers.

6 Lose your temper at work.

7 Drink alcohol at work.

8 Separate your private and professional life as far as possible.

9 Respect the views of others.

10 Act in a way that could put anyone at risk.

11 Be honest and constructive.

12 Ask if there is anything you are unsure about.

tip / tɪp / verb 1 **tip (sth) (up)** to move so that one side is higher than the other; to make sth move in that way: *When I stood up, the bench tipped up and the person on the other end fell off.* 2 to make sth come out of a container by holding or lifting it at an angle: *Tip the dirty water down the drain. The child tipped all the toys on to the floor.* 3 to give a waiter, etc. a small amount of extra money (in addition to the normal charge) to thank him / her: *She tipped the taxi driver generously.* 4 **tip sb/sth (as sth/to do sth)** to think or say that sb/sth is likely to do sth: *This horse is tipped to win the race. He is widely tipped as the next Prime Minister.*

Reading

Tips on tipping

1 Read the article and complete the table with the amount or percentage for each tip mentioned.

	Taxis	Restaurants
Belgium		
Czech Republic		
Denmark		
Egypt		
India		
Japan		

2 Read the article again. Write T (true) or F (false).

1 It's a good idea for tourists to find out about tipping before leaving home.

2 In India, you should tip a porter 10 rupees for carrying your bags.

3 If you are not sure how much to give, be generous.

4 Tipping is more or less the same in European countries.

3 Which piece of advice about tipping was the most surprising to you?

4 Which country in the article seems most like your country in terms of tipping?

How to tip in different countries

If you're travelling overseas on holiday this summer, the preparations may already seem overwhelming – so the last thing you're likely to worry about is tipping. You could regret that, however, once you're sitting in the back of a taxi, wondering how much to tip, if at all.

In India, for example, you could have saved yourself a headache by finding out beforehand that you should round the taxi fare up to the next 10 rupees and give porters 10 rupees a bag; if the concierge got you your taxi on your way out to dinner, he would appreciate five rupees; and at dinner it's appropriate to tip 10% of the bill, unless a service charge is included.

Tipping as an insult

Tipping in developing countries and Asia is perhaps the most confusing. Not only do customs vary hugely, but there are often ethical and cultural factors to consider. Keen to avoid an awkward situation, many tourists will be generous. However, this strategy might not be as acceptable as you would think.

In many cultures, for example particularly in Asian and Pacific countries such as Japan, tipping is actually perceived as an insult. You could even end up breaking the law – in Vietnam, tipping is illegal.

At the other end of the spectrum are countries where tipping is a way of life. The first word many travellers to Egypt learn is *baksheesh* (tip), and anyone dealing with or helping tourists will expect a small tip, say, 5 or 10%.

When travelling in Europe, it's easy to assume tipping customs will be the same everywhere. But this isn't necessarily so. Take restaurants. Some include service charges; others don't.

Even if there is a service charge, you may be expected to tip a little extra. In Denmark, tipping isn't expected in restaurants at all. In Belgium, Finland, Hungary, Iceland, Norway, Portugal, and Sweden, you should tip 10%, but only if there's no service charge. In Austria, the Czech Republic, France, Germany, Greece, Holland, Italy, Luxembourg, Spain, and Ukraine, you should tip 5% to 10%, even if there's a service charge.

Do your research

Researching tipping practices is relatively simple. There are …

Find out

1 Work with a partner.

1 Research tipping in your area. Find out how much tourism professionals expect to be tipped in different situations, including

   a a porter carrying your bag to / from the train
   b a taxi driver
   c in restaurants
   d a porter taking your bag to your hotel room
   e a hotel concierge for getting you tickets and bookings
   f the housekeeper who cleaned your room
   g a tour guide at the end of the tour
   h the bus driver at the end of the tour.

2 Include any other people who you might give a tip to in your area.

3 Check on the Internet to see if there is any advice for your area.

2 Tell the other members of the class what you found out.

3 Listen to the other members of your class. Note down any advice that you didn't already have.

Writing
Local 'tips'

Sunseeker Holidays

Getting the best from your holiday

Travelling can be one of life's great pleasures. But if you're away and you become unwell, or if you have something stolen, then your holiday can be spoiled completely. Sunseeker Holidays wants you to have the time of your life when you are at your destination. Because of this we have prepared a few simple precautions that you can take to make sure you have a really great time . . .

1 Work in pairs. Produce a leaflet giving tourists advice on health and safety. Include information on

- health and safety when sunbathing
- safety in the sea and around the swimming pool
- security when staying out late
- tipping in hotels, restaurants, taxis, etc.

2 Write an introduction for your leaflet like the one above.

Checklist

Assess your progress in this unit. Tick (✓) the statements which are true.

- ☐ I can understand people talking about the work of holiday representatives
- ☐ I can talk about the different skills and qualities holiday reps need
- ☐ I can prepare and give a welcome meeting talk to new groups
- ☐ I can understand texts talking about tipping when on holiday
- ☐ I can produce a leaflet giving advice on holiday health, safety, and tipping

Key words

Nouns	Adjectives
campsite courier	allergic
chalet host	bruised
clipboard	diabetic
diarrhoea	dizzy
entertainment	seasonal
health and safety checks	sore
rash	swollen
sunburn	unwell
throat	upset
toothache	variable

Verbs
socialize
tip

Next stop

1 When was the last time you ate out? What did you have?

2 Do you like eating local dishes when you are on holiday? Why (not)?

3 What's the nicest meal you've had as a tourist?

4 What's the strangest food you've ever eaten on holiday?

5 Eating out

Take off

a Mexico

b India

c Japan

d Turkey

e Peru

f Poland

1 **Match the different dishes with the flags.**

2 What is your country's national dish?

3 How would you describe this dish to somebody who didn't know what it was?

4 What three things would you recommend to a tourist about the food of your region?

Listening

Our national dish

1 🎧 Listen to three people talking about their national dish. Match them with the pictures and flags above.

2 Which of the three is happiest about their national dish?

3 Which of them is the least happy about their national dish?

4 Are you happy about your national dish?

5 If you could choose another dish to represent your country, which would it be?

Reading

Food tourism

1 Read the extracts about food tourism. Which title goes with which extract?

  1 A new type of tourist?
  2 Food tourism – a winner for everyone
  3 In celebration of basic food
  4 Sea, sand, sun – and food!

2 Think of a heading for the remaining extract.

3 Which extract(s) is / are

  1 publicity for a food event or festival?
  2 from an article for tourism professionals?
  3 from a web page describing a tourist region?

4 Read the extracts again. Write T (true) or F (false).

  1 At the end of the bakers' festival in the Philippines, the participants eat the bread.
  2 When you go to the chocolate festival in New York, you don't have to try the chocolate.
  3 'Tasters' are people who try local food when on holiday in Tasmania.
  4 The Central Dalmatia gastronomic guide is a list of all the restaurants in the country.

5 Which of the food festivals described sounds most attractive to you?

6 Which are the most important food festivals in your region?

In this unit
- food tourism
- describing dishes
- introducing the food of a region
- relative clauses
- dealing with complaints

a

Date:	2nd week of February
Name:	TINAPAY FESTIVAL
Venue:	Cuenca, Batangas, the Philippines

The Tinapay festival is an opportunity for the local people to give thanks to their patron saint, Our Lady of Peace and Good Voyage. In particular, the festival is an act of recognition of the wonderful breadmaking skills of the bakers of Cuenca. The main event is a unique parade where the biggest and longest breads of different shapes are paraded through the main streets of the town. And the festival is interactive – after the parade everyone gets a taste of the pastries and bread products.

b

It is important for tourism managers to realise that food tourism is not just good news for the tourist; local people also benefit from it. As one tourism expert pointed out, 'Hungry visitors mean good business, not only for our restauranteurs, but also for the farmers and fishermen who are their suppliers.'

c

Anybody looking for a truly heavenly experience will think that they have walked into paradise at the Chocolate Show in New York. The festival is a chocolate experience of global proportions with over 60 makes of chocolates on show. Chocolate-makers from all over the world take part, as do the visitors – chocolate tasting is mandatory!

d

A study in Tasmania has suggested that a new brand of food-lover exists. 'Tasters' are visitors who are interested in the food of a region as a part of their overall tourism experience. They are looking for the real taste of the area, for something representative and authentic, and they hope to find part of this in local food and wines.

e

Central Dalmatia is one of Croatia's regions that takes greatest pride in the quality and diversity of the dishes served on its islands and along its coasts. Recently this richness has become much more than a source of pleasure for the locals. Now it is a significant ingredient in what the region offers tourists. In fact, food is so important for tourism in Dalmatia that local experts have produced the region's first ever gastronomic guide.

Find out

Is food used as a tourism resource in your region? Find out

1   what the most representative dishes are for the food in your region

2   what the most common local ingredients are that are used in making these dishes

3   which of these dishes is used in local tourist festivals or offered by local restaurants.

(Hint: go to your local tourist information office, look at the menus of restaurants and hotel restaurants used by tourists, check on the Internet, or ask your family and friends.)

Food tourism has become big business, worth nearly £4bn a year. In a recent survey of the UK food industry, two-thirds of Britons said that food and drink influenced their holiday choice.

Vocabulary

Food: ingredients and preparation

1 Look at the food web. How is it organized?

2 Where would the ingredients go on the web?

3 Add any other ingredients that are used in the food of your region. Use your dictionary if necessary.

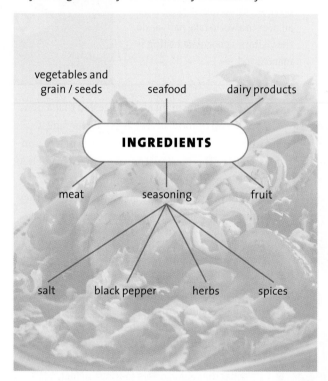

vegetables and grain / seeds · seafood · dairy products

INGREDIENTS

meat · seasoning · fruit

salt · black pepper · herbs · spices

aubergine	lamb	prawns
cheese	lobster	pulses
chicken	olive oil	rice
courgette	onion	sausage
crab	oranges	strawberries
cream	peppers	yogurt
garlic	pork	

4 Which of these methods of preparing food can you use with the different ingredients?

| 1 baked | 3 fried | 5 stewed |
| 2 boiled | 4 grilled | 6 stuffed |

5 Which of the ingredients would you normally use in
1 a starter
2 a main course
3 a dessert?

Pronunciation

1 🎧 Listen to the words at the top of each column. Pay attention to the vowel sound.

	sea	sort	spot
	/iː/	/ɔː/	/ɒ/
1 cheese			
2 courgette			
3 course			
4 cream			
5 lobster			
6 meat			
7 olive			
8 oranges			
9 pork			
10 prawns			

2 🎧 Listen to the food words and tick (✓) the right column for the vowel sound you hear.

3 🎧 Listen and repeat the words. Pay attention to the length of the vowel sounds.

4 Add any other food words you know to each column.

Listening

Describing dishes

1 🎧 Listen and tick (✓) the food that is being described.

2 🎧 Listen again. For each dish, make notes about
   1 ingredients   2 preparation   3 accompaniments.

3 Are the dishes being described starters, main courses, or desserts?

4 Which dish sounds nicest to you, and which dish would you least like to try?

● Language spot

Describing food

1 Look at what the waiters said (a–f). Identify phrases for
   1 giving a general idea of a dish
   2 describing the ingredients and preparation
   3 describing what accompanies the dish.

   a A salade Marocaine is made of chopped tomatoes.
   b Harira is a bit like tomato soup.
   c It's a type of stew.
   d It's cooked with potatoes and other vegetables.
   e Schnitzel is served with potato salad and a slice of lemon.
   f The meat is covered in breadcrumbs.

2 Which phrases use the passive voice?

3 Look at the waiter's English notes on the Malaysian dish Nasi Lemak. What would the waiter actually say to the guest?

> 1 very special Malaysian dish
> 2 typically eaten: breakfast
> 3 served here: evening
> 4 ingredients = rice & coconut cream
> 5 like rice pudding but not dessert
> 6 rice soaked in coconut cream
> 7 rice & cream steamed + herbs
> 8 served + cucumber, anchovies, peanuts

>> Go to **Grammar reference** p.121

Speaking

Taking an order

1 Look at these phrases. In what order would a waiter use them during a meal?
   1 Are you ready to order?
   2 Enjoy your meal.
   3 Good evening. A table for two?
   4 Here's the menu. Today's special is …
   5 This way, please.
   6 Would you like to order some wine with your meal?
   7 Can I get you an aperitif?

2 Work in pairs. Student A, you are the customer. Student B, you are the waiter. Go to p.131 and choose one of the situations from *Listening*.

3 Act out the restaurant situation. The waiter should use phrases from *Language spot*.

4 Now change roles. Act out the other situation.

5 Think of your local dishes. Choose a starter, a main course, and a dessert.

6 Act out a restaurant situation. Student A, you are a visitor to B's region. Student B, you are the waiter. Try to describe the dishes.

7 Now think of some different dishes. Change roles and act out the restaurant situation.

complement (n) a thing that goes together well with sth else

savoury (adj) having a taste that is not sweet

self-sufficient (adj) able to produce or provide everything that you need without help from or having to buy from others

skewer (n) a long, thin piece of pointed metal or wood that is pushed through pieces of meat, vegetables, etc. to hold them together while they are cooking

Reading
The traveller's guide to Turkish food

1 Climate can influence the food of a region. What other influences can you think of?

2 What do you think are the main influences on Turkish food? Read the first two paragraphs to check.

3 Read the article again. Write T (true) or F (false).

1 Because of the climate, you get different dishes at different times of the year.

2 Mezes are put in the centre of the table for everybody to try.

3 Turkish meals usually take a long time.

4 Lamb or chicken with tasty rice are typical mezes.

5 It is quite common for Turkish people to have their main course in one restaurant and their sweet course in another.

6 Turkish people don't like sweet food.

4 What do you think 'Afiyet olsun' means?

TURKISH CUISINE

Turkish food is delicious, rich, and varied. Turkey is **self-sufficient** in food, and the range of vegetables and fruits available at all times of the year provides a constant source of fresh ingredients. Because of this, the taste and preparation of the wide range of dishes changes with the seasons. We never use tinned or frozen ingredients, unless it is to create a specific taste.

Turkish food has some of its origins in the lifestyle of the people that lived in this region during the time of the Sultans. Even today the evening meal is often the evening's entertainment. The equivalent of the western 'starter' is mezes, which consist of a huge selection of tasty dishes served in the centre of the table, including vegetables, meat, chicken, and seafood all prepared differently. Everyone tastes all of the dishes, which often consist of the same

vegetable prepared in a number of very different ways. There are, for example, over 100 ways to prepare aubergines alone.

Eating at home in Turkey or in a traditional Turkish restaurant is never hurried, and the evening meal can last for many hours. The transition from starters to the main course is not always obvious, but typical main course dishes are **skewers** of succulent lamb or chicken, accompanied by tasty rice dishes.

Desserts are extremely sweet and the perfect **complement** to the strongly savoury aspect of Turkish food. The wide range of sweet dishes available is a good complement to the equally extensive range of mezes. Visitors to Turkey are often surprised by an unusual Turkish custom. When you eat out, it is not unusual to change restaurants at the dessert stage!

● Language spot

Relative clauses – *who, which,* and *that*

1 Look at these sentences. When do we use *who* and when do we use *which*?

> Hungry visitors mean good business, not only for our restauranteurs, but also for the farmers and fishermen <u>who</u> are their suppliers.
>
> 'Tasters' are visitors <u>who</u> are interested in the food of a region as a part of their overall tourism experience.
>
> I really love our food, especially sushi, <u>which</u> is our national dish.
>
> The equivalent of the western 'starter' is mezes, <u>which</u> consist of a huge selection of tasty dishes …

>> Go to **Grammar reference** p.121

2 Now look at these sentences. When do we use *which* and when do we use *that*?

> Turkish food has some of its origins in the lifestyle of the people <u>that</u> lived in this region during the time of the Sultans.
>
> The equivalent of the western 'starter' is mezes, <u>which</u> consist of a huge selection of tasty dishes …
>
> Everyone tastes all of the dishes, <u>which</u> often consist of the same vegetable prepared in a number of very different ways.
>
> Tagines are the pots <u>that</u> the dish is cooked in.
>
> It's rice <u>that</u> has been soaked in coconut cream and then steamed with some herbs.

>> Go to **Grammar reference** p.121

> We hope this short culinary guide provides you with an insight into eating in Turkey and gives you another reason to visit this very hospitable country. It only remains to wish you a very sincere, 'Afiyet olsun'.

3 Complete the sentences with *who, which,* or *that.*

1 The dish _____ most visitors associate with the UK is fish and chips.

2 The Mediterranean diet, _____ is based on olive oil, is now considered to be very healthy.

3 Foods _____ are frozen or tinned are never as tasty as fresh foods.

4 *Foodies* is a name used today in the UK for people _____ really enjoy eating.

5 Turkey, _____ is where Europe meets Asia, is an important bridge between cultures.

6 Gourmets and epicureans are people _____ see food as a serious hobby.

Writing

The food of my region

1 Work with a partner. You are going to write an introduction to the food of your country or region. Use the information you gathered for *Find out*. Add other information if necessary.

2 Think about what you can say about each of the following aspects of your local food.

1 the influences
2 the history
3 the ingredients and flavours
4 the importance for local culture and lifestyle
5 the way of eating a meal
6 the most representative dishes

3 Look at the article on Turkish food. How many paragraphs does it have? How many paragraphs will your article need?

4 When you have written a first draft for your article, give it to your teacher to correct.

5 While you are waiting to get your first draft back, think about how you can best present your article – as a web page, as a leaflet, etc.

Where in the world?

Toronto's *360 Restaurant* is one of Canada's top restaurants – in more than one way! How is it a 'top' restaurant? And what's different about its cellar?

360 The Restaurant at the CN Tower

360 The Restaurant at the CN Tower, one of Toronto's finest and most popular restaurants, features unforgettable food combined with a magnificent revolving view of Toronto more than 350 metres below. *360* offers market-fresh cuisine, featuring regional ingredients to ensure an incomparable culinary experience.

All seats offer a breathtaking view. Some are located against the window and others are on a raised platform. All seats in the restaurant are on the rotating floor and receive spectacular 360 degree views. The floor takes 72 minutes to complete a full rotation.

At 351 metres, our cellar has received a Guinness World Record for the world's highest wine cellar. Created to resemble a typical underground wine cellar, ours features precision climate and humidity controls, redwood racks, double cherry doors, a 9,000-bottle storage capacity, and a tasting table. Our 'cellar in the sky' has an award-winning wine selection of over 550 international and Canadian wines. *360* is the recipient of several awards and a wonderful place to celebrate any special occasion.

Elevation from ground level to the restaurant is complimentary with the purchase of a main course. Reservations are recommended and can be made online or by calling 416-362-5411.

Customer care
What do you say?

Most languages have common expressions which are said on certain occasions, e.g. in French, 'bon appetit' to guests at a dinner table, or 'bon voyage' to travellers before a trip. English often does not have simple equivalents to these expressions and sometimes borrows from other languages. So, before a meal the English will probably either say 'bon appetit' or possibly 'enjoy your meal' – or sometimes nothing at all.

In what situations are these other common expressions used?

1 'Safe journey'   2 'You're welcome'   3 'Do start'   4 'Cheers'   5 'Have a nice day'

Listening

How to deal with complaints

1 Look at the four steps for dealing with customer complaints. What order do you think these steps normally come in?

Apologize   Ask questions   Listen   Take action

2 🎧 Listen to the head waiter giving a final training talk in a restaurant and check your answer.

3 Why should tourism professionals be 'positive' about getting complaints?

4 How can you 'show the customer that you're listening'?

5 When is it essential to ask the customer questions?

6 In the talk, three phrases for apologizing are given. What are they?

7 What do you think customers complain about most in restaurants?

Speaking

I'm *very* sorry

1 Work in threes. Student A, you are the waiter. Go to p.108. Student B, you are the customer. Go to p.110. Student C, you are the training manager. Use the evaluation form below to assess the waiter.

2 Act out the complaints. Change roles so that everybody is the waiter at least twice.

1	Did the waiter fully understand the customer at all times?	Y / ? / N
2	Did the waiter show the customer that they were listening?	Y / ? / N
3	Did the waiter apologize using appropriate language?	Y / ? / N
4	Did the waiter's voice clearly express sincerity in the apology?	Y / ? / N
5	Did the waiter offer an appropriate solution to the problem?	Y / ? / N

Checklist

Assess your progress in this unit. Tick (✓) the statements which are true.

- ☐ I can understand articles about food tourism and local food
- ☐ I can use basic vocabulary to talk about the ingredients and preparation of different dishes
- ☐ I can describe local dishes to a customer in a restaurant
- ☐ I can write an introduction to the food of my country / region
- ☐ I can deal with simple problems in a restaurant

Key words

Ingredients	Other
beef	course
garlic	dessert
lamb	dish
olive oil	flavour
pepper	main course
pork	starter
prawn	taste
pulses	
sausage	
spices	
yogurt	

Preparation
baked
grilled
stewed
stuffed

Next stop

1 Have you or any of your friends ever had a holiday in the countryside?

2 Where did you go and what activities were you able to do?

3 Which do you prefer – holidays in the countryside, city holidays, or beach holidays?

4 Which do your parents prefer?

6 Rural tourism

Take off

1 Look at the pictures of different tourist activities. What can you see in each picture?

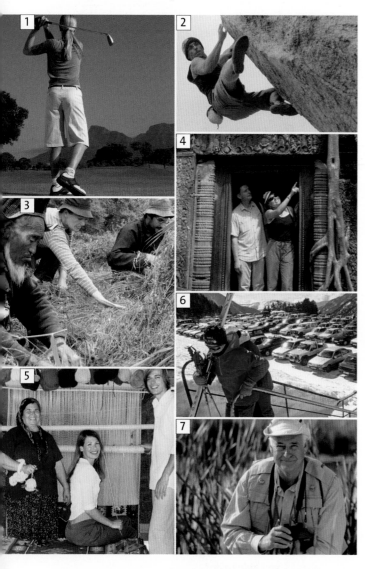

2 Work in groups. Which pictures show people participating in rural tourism activities? Explain your answers to your partners.

3 Name three other activities that are typical of rural tourism.

4 Try to produce a simple definition of what rural tourism is. Share your definition with the rest of the class.

Listening

Local people and rural tourism

1 Say which activities in *Take off* **1** involve these people.

a — a guide for a monument
b — a warden for a nature reserve
c — an outdoor activities instructor
d — a local crafts worker

2 🎧 Listen to three of the people in **1** talking about rural tourism. Identify each speaker.

3 Which speaker
1 has a formal tourism qualification?
2 is carrying on the work their parents did?
3 thinks that their area has a lot of different activities to offer rural tourism visitors?

4 🎧 Listen again and make notes about the way(s) each speaker or their region has benefited from rural tourism.

5 We didn't hear one person speak. What do you think they would say about rural tourism? (Hint: think about how tourism will affect their job.)

It's my job

Eduardo Barroso

Eduardo was born in a remote village in the Atacama Desert in the north of Chile. Life in the desert is hard, but rural tourism has given Eduardo and his family the chance to make a living from their surroundings. What is there to attract people to the desert? What is there to do there? Where do people stay? Read on and find out.

How did you decide to start up in rural tourism?
Life here is not easy, so many young people from the villages go to Santiago to find work. I wanted to be with my family, and one day my father read about rural tourism in Europe and decided to do the same with our farm.

Why do people visit the Atacama? What's the attraction?
The landscape is the obvious attraction. For people from the city, there's the shock of how big and empty the desert is. And for people from a temperate climate, there's the surprise of how beautiful and varied it can be.

Is the desert varied?
It certainly isn't just sand, which is the image in most people's minds. In the Atacama, for example, you have volcanoes, salt lakes, geysers, canyons … It's much more than just sand.

But what can you do here apart from look at the landscape?
My family have worked this land as farmers for many years, and we still do, so one of the attractions for our visitors is to experience our daily life. On the first morning, visitors help us around the farm, milking cows or putting the sheep out to graze. We have bees, as well.

You are very proud of the accommodation you have. Can you tell us why?
All of the buildings are made in traditional style and from local materials. Straw, mud, stone … everything is from the *Patta Hoiri*. That's 'Mother Earth' in our local language. And all of the food we give visitors is based on ancient recipes and local ingredients. It might not be as sophisticated as in the best restaurants of Santiago, but it is tasty and very healthy. But perhaps the thing our guests enjoy most is that they dine with us. And after every meal there is always time for a *tertulia* – an after-dinner chat that often goes on long into the night. That's when they really feel part of our world, and that's what rural tourism is about for us.

Find out

1 Choose a country that offers rural tourism. Find out
   1 how long there has been rural tourism
   2 what sort of accommodation is available
   3 what types of activities visitors can do
   4 when the high and low seasons are
   5 if there are any professional associations of rural tourism.

2 Make a brief report of your findings.

carve (v) cut wood or stone in order to make an object or to put a pattern or writing on it

comply with (v) to obey an order or request

continental breakfast (n) a light breakfast, usually consisting of coffee and bread rolls with butter and jam

full cooked breakfast (n) a large breakfast, usually consisting of cereal, cooked bacon and eggs, toast, and tea or coffee

Reading

Ask someone who has been there

Newspapers often have travel supplements and invite readers to answer questions other readers send in. Here, four readers answer a question by Alison.

1 Look at the pictures. What do you think Alison's question is about?

2 Read the question. Were you right?

3 Now read the answers and
   1 match pictures a–f with the countries mentioned
   2 make a list of the different factors that the different systems take into account when describing each grade
   3 think of three other factors that you could use in a grading system.

4 Which system is the best in your opinion?

Q | **Dear Fellow Travellers**

The English Tourist Board uses crowns to grade serviced accommodation and keys for self-catering. Does anybody know what systems are used for rural accommodation in other places?

Alison, Penrith

A | **Dear Alison**

We've just got back from New Zealand. They use a system called Qualmark, which operates on a 1- to 5-star scale. One star means 'Acceptable'. In practice, this means it meets your basic needs and is clean and comfortable. We stayed in a lot of three-star places and they were good.

Dave & Jane Walcott, Weston-super-Mare

A | **Dear Alison**

We often go to the Isle of Man. There they use a diamond to grade guest house accommodation. As it says on the offcial government web

page (www.gov.im/tourism/travel/accommodation/isle-of-man-hotels.aspx), one diamond means you'll get *'Clean and comfortable accommodation. Offering a **full cooked** or **continental** breakfast. Acceptable level of quality and helpful service'.* At the top end of the range, five diamonds means *'An excellent overall level of quality. Excellent interior design, high quality furniture, and an excellent quality bed. Breakfast offering wide choice of high quality fresh ingredients. Excellent levels of customer care.'*

Keith & Anne, Harrow

A | **Dear Alison**

Here in Romania, rural accommodation in guest houses is classified in accordance with the law. The system goes from one daisy to five daisies. In the past we used stars (and our hotels here still do), but recently we chose daisies for guest houses in the country because it is a flower that grows all over Romania.

Kindest regards

Ecaterina, Bucovina

A | **Dear Alison**

Here in Japan we have no accommodation grading system.

Motoko, Tokyo

A | **Dear Alison**

In Asturias in the north of Spain, we use a symbol we call the 'trisquel' for grading our 'casas de aldea' (village houses). This is a traditional Celtic symbol, and you can see it **carved** in many old buildings in our region. The system goes from one to three 'trisquels'. To get three, the accommodation has to **comply with** very high standards of quality and functionality. For example, the owner must be in the village all the time, there should be good access for disabled travellers, the furniture and decorations should be traditional in style and materials, there should be a children's play area, and so on.

Onofre Alvarez Fernández, Sociedad Regional de Turismo de Asturias

Listening

Checking in at a campsite

1 🎧 Listen to two situations in which campers check in to a campsite. Which camper

  a has made a previous reservation?
  b has a vehicle?
  c is staying for less than a week?
  d has children?
  e only needs one pitch?

2 Look at the campsite symbols. Do you know what they mean? Which ones correspond to which situation in **1**?

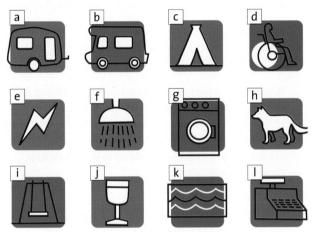

3 🎧 Listen again and complete the sentences.

  1 And it's _____ _____ for a
    motorhome and a _____ _____ for a
    family tent.

  2 Could you _____ _____ _____
    _____ for a moment?

  3 Will you be using an _____ _____ ?

  4 OK. _____ _____ _____
    _____ here, please?

  5 We've got _____ _____ _____
    Friday.

  6 What were you _____ _____ ?

Pronunciation

1 🎧 Listen to these phrases from situation 1. Note how the words in *italics* in each phrase are stressed.

Receptionist	Here you are. Two adults, two children, two weeks. And it's one pitch for a *motorhome*, and a *second* pitch for a family *tent*.
Camper 1	Two pitches, that's right. But it's not a *family* tent. It's a *small* tent – for the *children*.
Receptionist	Oh. I'll just change it. There you are. One *motor*home and one *small* tent.

2 Which words are stressed in order to *confirm* information that is right, and which are stressed to *correct* information that is wrong?

3 🎧 Now look at these phrases from situation 2. Decide which word will be stressed in each of the phrases underlined, then listen and check.

Camper 2	There are four of us. We've got tents.
Receptionist	Are they family tents?
Camper 2	No, no. They're small tents. They're mountain tents.
Receptionist	And is that four tents?
Camper 2	No. Only two.
Receptionist	Have you got a car?
Camper 2	No, we've got bikes.
Receptionist	Motorbikes?
Camper	No, they're normal bikes. You know, pedal bikes.

Speaking

Receiving campers

1 Work in pairs. Student A, you are the receptionist. Go to p.110. Student B, you are the camper. Go to p.115. Act out the situation. Use the phrases in *Listening* **3**, and remember to stress any important words.

2 Now change roles and act out the second situation.

3 If you want to know how good your pronunciation is, record one of the two situations and give it to your teacher to assess.

Rural tourism is a segment of the total tourist industry which is particularly important in Hungary, a country with no spectacular natural attractions, without seaside, high mountains, rainforest, or herds of exotic animals.

Vocabulary

Resources for rural tourism

1 Look at these different resources for rural tourism. Which ones do you recognize?

1	birdwatching	10	orchards
2	brewing	11	pottery
3	cycling	12	traditional crafts
4	farms	13	trekking
5	fishing villages	14	waterfall
6	forests	15	watermill
7	landscape	16	weaving
8	lifestyle	17	wildlife
9	meadows	18	woodcarving

2 Which of the resources in **1** can be classified as

a activities that show tourists local culture?

b activities that show tourists the local natural environment?

c something for tourist to watch?

d something for tourists to do?

3 Think of two more resources for each category in **2**.

4 Which of the resources can you find in your country?

5 Which of the resources have you had any experience of?

Reading

Welcome!

1 Work with a partner. Look at the photos of life in rural Vietnam.

1 Use the vocabulary of rural tourism resources to describe what is happening in each photo.

2 Can you think of any other rural tourism activities that you might find in Vietnam?

2 Read the article welcoming tourists and look at the map.

1 Identify the provinces of Vinh Long, Quang Nam, and Bac Ninh on the map.

2 Match the photos with the corresponding provinces.

Welcome to rural Vietnam

Welcome to a corner of Asia where you will find a lifestyle that goes back for centuries. Fishing on the Mekong Delta, farming in Central Vietnam, or crafts in Bac Ninh Province – whatever your own interest, we are sure you will find something to **delight** you in rural Vietnam.

Vinh Long Province

Located between the Tien and Hau rivers, the fertile lands of Vinh Long **nourish** thousands of fruit orchards, while the countless small islands provide ideal conditions for ecotourism and observing wildlife.

In addition, you will be able to observe the centuries-old activities of Southern Vietnam, such as processing rice paper and traditional Vietnamese cooking.

Especially interesting in Vinh Long is the opportunity to stay overnight in local residents' homes. There is a small but growing number of privates homes that offer home stays. At the moment they provide accommodation and entertainment for up to 150 tourists per night.

delight (v) to give sb great pleasure

nourish (v) to give sb / sth the right kind of food so that he / she / it can grow and be healthy

silkworm (n) a caterpillar (a small creature like a worm with legs) that produces silk thread

toil (v) to work very hard and / or for a long time

trade (n) the activity of buying and selling or of exchanging goods or services between people or countries

---

3 Which of the provinces is best for visitors who want to
  1 do things during their stay in rural Vietnam?
  2 get as close as possible to ordinary Vietnamese people?
  3 buy authentic souvenirs of rural Vietnamese products?

4 Which area of Vietnam seems the most exciting to you? Tell your partner why.

5 Where would you find a text like this?

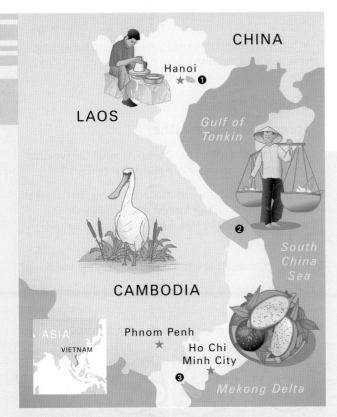

Quang Nam Province

For visitors who want to be really active in their holidays, we recommend a visit to one of the vegetable farming villages near the town of Hoi An in the central province of Quang Nam. Here for a day you can **toil** shoulder to shoulder with a Vietnamese farmer. Hosts and guests work the land, planting rice or collecting vegetables that they sell in the local markets. For lunch you get to eat colocynth (similar to a bitter apple) and tom huu, which is a traditional dish made of vegetables.

Writing

Welcome – Bienvenue – Willkommen

With so many places to visit, a Welcome text is important for rural areas. Work with a partner. You are going to write a Welcome text.

1 With your partner, make notes.
  1 Which elements of rural tourism are typical of your area?
  2 Which adjectives will help you to describe your region and make it sound unique?
  3 Which images can you use to illustrate your text?

2 Work on your own. Write your text. When you have finished, give it to your partner to read.

3 Work together. Use the best of your individual texts to produce the best Welcome text you can. Did you use adjectives to make the region sound special?

Bac Ninh Province

The homeland of Quan Ho art has many traditional **trade** villages. In Xuan Lai village you can find excellent bamboo products, especially from black bamboo, while Phu Lang is famous for its pottery. Thousands of ancient pots have been found here, and even today there are about 300 families in the village doing pottery work.

Tho Ha is famous for pottery, but nowadays it has also started to produce wine. Another village that is well-known for traditional wines is Van, on the bank of the Cau River.

The villagers here are happy to let visitors photograph their wine being made, and to try it or to buy it, but the brewing process itself is a secret.

Finally, Da Hoi is a must. This 400-year-old trade village is famous for its traditional silk cloth, and women there still raise **silkworms** and weave fabulous fabrics that they sell.

Customer care

Encouraging customers to be sensitive to the environment

There is a piece of advice that responsible tourism organizations often give to travellers: 'Take only photographs; leave only footprints.'

1 What are they encouraging their customers *not* to leave, and *not* to take?

The Countryside Code encourages tourists to be responsible to the rural environment in the UK. The key points are

- Be safe, plan ahead, and follow any signs.
- Leave gates and property as you find them.
- Protect plants and animals and take your litter home.
- Keep dogs under close control.
- Consider other people.

2 Would you change anything for a countryside code for the rural environment in your country?

3 What points would you include for a code for the *urban* environment in your country?

Vocabulary

Weather words

1 Match the weather terms a–l with pictures 1–12.

a	clear and bright	g	light winds
b	cloudy	h	overcast
c	heavy rain	i	storms
d	heavy showers	j	strong winds
e	light rain	k	sunny intervals
f	light showers	l	thundery showers

2 What other weather words can you add?

3 Which words in **1** are typical of (a) good and (b) bad weather?

4 *Thundery* is an adjective. The noun is *thunder*. What are the adjectives for

1	fog?	3	mist?	5	storms?
2	rain?	4	showers?	6	wind?

5 Make a web for all your weather terms similar to the web you made for food vocabulary in Unit 5. Put the words *Weather forecast* in the centre of your web.

6 What is the weather like in your region in the spring, summer, and autumn?

Listening

Forecasting the weather

In rural areas, visitors need to know what the weather will be like so that they can plan what to do.

1 🎧 Listen to a rural accommodation owner in Cornwall, England. She is telling a guest about the weather. What is the weather forecast for (a) tomorrow and (b) Thursday?

2 What is the weather like at the time they are speaking?

3 Why is tomorrow afternoon going to be different from today?

4 Why does the owner tell the visitor not to worry?

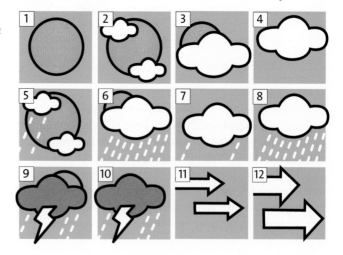

● Language spot

Making predictions

1 🎧 Listen to the dialogue in *Listening* again and complete the phrases.

1 Do you know what the weather _____ _____ _____ tomorrow?

2 (I think) _____ _____ _____ today.

3 ... then _____ _____ again in the afternoon.

4 I think _____ _____ a few thundery storms.

5 Will it _____ _____ _____ all week?

6 They said _____ _____ _____ rain on Thursday.

2 Which two verbs forms can you use when you are giving information about the weather? Which is the more common of the two forms?

3 Which is more certain?

1 *It'll be like today* or *It'll probably be like today.*

2 *I think it'll rain on Thursday* or *It's going to rain on Thursday.*

>> Go to **Grammar reference** p.122

Speaking

Giving information about the weather

1 Work in pairs. Student A, go to p.109. Use the information to give the camper a weather forecast for the next four days. Student B, you are the camper.

EXAMPLE

Camper   *Excuse me. Do you know what the weather will be like for the next few days?*

Receptionist   *Well, for tomorrow I think it'll ...*

2 When you have finished, change roles. Student A, you are the camper. Student B, go to p.112. Use the information to give the weather forecast.

Checklist

Assess your progress in this unit. Tick (✓) the statements which are true.

- ☐ I can understand people talking about what rural tourism is
- ☐ I can understand rural accommodation grading systems
- ☐ I can check campers into a campsite
- ☐ I can write a welcome text describing rural tourism in a region
- ☐ I can give a simple weather forecast

Key words

Accommodation	Weather
electric hook-up	fog
grading system	forecast
home stay	overcast
motorhome	shower
pitch	storm
symbol	sunny intervals
	thunder

Rural attractions
canyon
cloth
crafts worker
forest
meadow
pottery
warden
weaving
woodcarving

Next stop

1 What is the most interesting tourist attraction you have visited? Why was it interesting?

2 Have you ever taken part in a festival or major public event?

3 What do you think are the three best tourist attractions in your country?

Writing bank

1 Report writing

1 Read the report and answer the questions.

1 Who wrote the report?

2 Who is going to read and use the report?

3 How did the writers collect the information?

4 Is the report positive or negative about online and multimedia tourist information in Dublin? Find examples of adjectives used which support your answer.

5 The writers were unable to find out much about one of the three main areas of information. Which one?

6 Which of the multimedia features do you think would be most useful for someone who (a) is planning to visit Dublin, and (b) has visited Dublin and has happy memories?

2 Here are some more items that might appear in the report. In which section would you put them?

1 Touch screen displays at the Tourist Information Centres were very popular with visitors

2 Talk to colleagues – with handout of report

3 Set up an email interview with the Director of Tourism Information Services for Dublin

4 Prepare PowerPoint slide presentation

Have a clear title.

Title
Dublin: Online and multimedia tourist information

Use full names of all authors.

Author(s)
Rahel de Jong and Christian Koller

Think about who you are writing the report for.

Report to
Managers of local TIC and other tourism decision-makers

Think about the aims of the report. Note the use of to (infinitive of purpose) at the start.

Purpose
To investigate the online and multimedia tourist information facilities provided by a typical European capital city tourist destination, with a view to the development and improvement of similar facilities in our own local Tourist Information services.

Use numbers and bullet points for sub-lists. Note the use of the Passive – it makes the report sound more formal.

Methodology

1 Information was collected from various sources, namely:

Internet search engines (e.g. Google, Yahoo) on key words: *Dublin tourist information multimedia*

Tourist Offices Worldwide Directory (www.towd.com)

Visit to local TIC for ideas.

2 Relevant information for report was then selected and ordered.

3 Report, including summary, was written.

Acknowledge all sources.

Sources used
The following sources were particularly useful in compiling this report:

www.visitdublin.com (especially the link to 'multimedia')

www.tourist-information-dublin.co.uk

Limit summary to two or three sentences.

Summary of findings
Dublin has excellent internet / online information for tourists and a good range of multimedia facilities. This fits with its image as a lively city blending the modern and the traditional. Tourist Information Centres in the city do not appear to be so well presented or accessible.

Details

1 Online Tourist Office

The Online Tourist Office was visually very attractive. It was very easy to click through to a wide range of useful information. In particular there were links to: *Accommodation finder, Entertainment, Events, See and do, Special offers,* and *Travel*. Text in all these sections was comprehensive without being too long. Photographs and design features were very effective. We particularly liked the 'maps' section and the section on 'information on travel', which gave details of discount passes.

2 Multimedia facilities

There were a number of useful multimedia features:

- e-cards – allows you to send electronic postcards from Dublin to your friends
- podcasts – free downloads providing audio-guides to various parts of Dublin
- screensavers – free download images of Dublin for your computer screensaver
- video – Dublin Tourism's promotional DVD with backing track, which can be watched before the visitor arrives, or when the tourist is deciding where to go
- webcam – gives real-time live footage of Dublin city centre, and can be used, for example, to watch the St Patrick's Day Parade wherever you are in the world.

All these features are not only useful for the visitor, but are also excellent ways of promoting Dublin as a destination.

3 Facilities at the TIC

No information was found about interactive and multimedia facilities at the central Dublin Tourist Information Centre. An email has been sent requesting this information, but no reply has been received.

Follow-up work

Prepare proposals for how some of the Dublin features might be included in our own regional tourist information services.

Mode of presentation

Written report to be emailed to relevant people.
Possibility for PowerPoint presentation using web slides.

Numbering the paragraphs of the 'detailed report' section, and using bullet points where appropriate, helps make the report clearer.

Give your own opinion of things you liked or didn't like.

It's OK to identify areas you haven't been able to find out about.

Put report in context of further work.

Think about how you will present the report. Try to think of interesting ways.

---

3 Here are some informal expressions used by the report writers when they were preparing the report. Find their more formal equivalents in the text.

1 The first thing we're going to do is collect as much information as possible.

2 We thought these websites were great.

3 The Tourist Information Centres didn't seem to be very easy to use.

4 What's good is that they get all the information in but still keep it short.

5 I think the next thing to do is make some suggestions for our local office.

4 What is the main tense used in the report? Find examples of the tense in both active and passive voice.

5 Prepare a similar report on one of the following.

- Online and multimedia tourist information in your region
- Hotel facilities for disabled people in an area of your choice
- Specialized holidays for the elderly
- Feedback from customers
- A research subject of your own choice related to tourism

2 Information leaflet

1 Read the leaflet and find this information.

1   time from airport to centre

2   the location of the Hong Kong Tourism Office

3   a traditional lunch dish

4   the location of two night markets

5   a place for a good view of the city

6   a fashionable place for dinner

7   opening hours of the temple

2 Find examples of these standard features for an information leaflet, and answer the questions.

1   Clear main heading. Does it indicate what the leaflet is about?

2   Strapline (or sub-heading) under the main heading: Is it more or less 'promotional' than the rest of the leaflet?

3   Section headings. Are they easy to see and do they indicate the content of the section?

4   Further information sources. What sources of information are given?

3 The grammar used in the leaflet is quite simple, for example, the Present Simple tense is used a lot (e.g. *Hong Kong consists of two parts*).

1   Find an example of the Present Simple in each section.

2   Find three examples of *can + infinitive*.

3   Find three examples of imperatives.

4 Write a similar leaflet for '48 hours in *[your city or a place you know well]*'.

---

48 HOURS IN HONG KONG

Discover the delights of China's most exciting city in a weekend

Getting there

Cathay Pacific, Qantas, British Airways, Virgin, and many other airlines fly non-stop to Hong Kong. From Chek Lap Kok, the Airport Express rail link (00 852 2881 8888; www.hongkongairport.com) takes you to the centre in 25 minutes.

Get your bearings

Hong Kong consists of two parts: Hong Kong Island and Kowloon, separated by Victoria Harbour. Both parts have modern hotels, shopping malls, and restaurants, but Kowloon has the best view – the steel towers of Hong Kong Island silhouetted against the wooded slopes of Victoria Peak. The two parts are linked by an efficient public rail system, road tunnels, and the famous Star Ferry.

Check in

Accommodation in Hong Kong can be expensive, with luxury hotels such as the Landmark Mandarin Oriental (00 852 2132 0188; www.mandarinoriental.com) and the famous Peninsula Hotel (www.peninsula.com). The Hong Kong Tourism Office in the Star Ferry Terminal Building (00 852 2508 1234; www.discoverhongkong.com) can help with other options.

Take a walk

The Dragon's Back, a ridge along the south-eastern side of Hong Kong Island, is an easy and popular hiking trail. The trek ends in the little fishing village of Shek O with its sandy beach and alfresco restaurants. Take the bus back to the city centre.

Lunch on the run

Dim sum is a Chinese institution. One of the oldest and best places to go is the Luk Yu Tea House on Stanley Street. The customers are mostly Chinese and you can watch the old women playing mah-jong.

Window shopping

Modern shopping malls are all over the city, or you can look for antiques at Hollywood Road. And of course there are the fabulous night markets in Kowloon: Temple Street and Ladies' Market in Mong Kok.

Take a view

The Peak Tram (00 852 2522 0922; www.thepeak.com.hk) makes a near vertical climb from Garden Road to the top of Victoria Peak for an amazing view across the city.

Dinner with the locals

Most locals head for the buzzing restaurants and bars on the streets of SoHo, or there are the Italian, Chinese, and Turkish eateries of Knutsford Terrace in Kowloon. The hottest place at the moment is Opia in the Jia Hotel (00 852 3196 9000; www.jiahongkong.com).

Sunday morning: go to the temple

A good place to feel the religious atmosphere and breathe in the incense smoke is Man Mo Temple on Hollywood Road, open daily from 8.00 a.m. to 6.00 p.m.

3 Public notices

Read texts A and B. They are about a sudden change of plans for a group of tourists.

1 What has happened to make the rep change plans?

2 What were the group going to do?

3 What are they going to do now?

4 What did the rep forget to tell his clients?

5 Which text was put on the campsite noticeboard? How do you know this?

6 Write a public notice telling people about the unexpected change in text C.

A   SPANISH ISLES

Mario

Change of plans for Wednesday, I'm afraid. Forecasting some really stormy weather – the tail of Hurricane Rita – tropical rain, high winds, waves & v. rough seas. Not good weather for camping. Especially bad for trips in glass-bottomed boats and up Teide mountain.

Need to re-schedule both trips. Will come across tomorrow morning and do this with you. Meanwhile get a notice out cancelling. Offer alternative of usual coach to Puerto de la Cruz for shopping.

Best

Rosa

P.S. And warn all to prepare tents, etc. for wind.

B   SPANISH ISLES CAMPING

BAD WEATHER WARNING & CHANGE OF PLANS

We have just received a warning for unexpected storms for Wednesday and Thursday. The storms are the remains of Hurricane Rita and for the Canary Islands they will mean high winds and very rough seas.

Because of this, and with your safety and security in mind, we have had to cancel

- all sea trips, including coastal cruises & glass-bottomed boats
- the Teide mountain summit trip.

We will be putting on coaches to Puerto de la Cruz for shopping & sightseeing on both days as an alternative activity. We will re-schedule both the sea trips and the Teide summit as soon as the weather calms down.

Please sign the list below if you are affected by these cancellations and wish to go to Puerto de la Cruz. Please contact us at the office if you have any questions.

Many thanks for your understanding.

Mario de la Fuente

Campsite rep

Spanish Isles Camping

C   SPANISH ISLES

Gisella

You're not going to believe it. A plague of jellyfish because the sea is very warm this year. It's no joke. 50 people treated for stings last week. Obviously the planned beach day for next Thursday no longer a good idea, especially for families. In fact, we need to think about re-scheduling all beach days for rest of summer.

Suggest we offer trip to local theme park – Acualandia or whatever it's called. Good for families, but we need them to reserve in advance through the office so that we can block-book entry tickets. For non-families suggest a trip to inland area – wine growing, wine tasting, village culture, etc. Will also need reservations. Can you get a notice up ASAP? Will ring you.

Alba

4 Email job application

Marta has found a website with hotel job vacancies. As part of the online application, she has to write a covering letter and send her CV.

1 Read Marta's letter. Which of the following points has she included?

1 age
2 education and qualifications
3 email address
4 interests
5 language skills
6 marital status
7 personality
8 work experience

2 How does Marta begin and close her letter?

3 Look at Marta's CV.

1 Where does she study?
2 Where does she live when she is not studying?
3 What relevant skills and job experience does Marta have?
4 Why does she put the most recent qualifications and experience first?

4 Compare Marta's letter with her CV. How has she adapted the letter to the job she is seeking?

5 Prepare your own CV using Marta's as a model.

6 Read the job advert and write a letter applying for the job.

Apply here for this job

Email address _____

Cover letter

Write your cover letter in the Apply Online box below. When you are ready, click on the Apply Online button.

Dear *Hotelwork4U*

I am writing to apply for the job of hotel receptionist, reference Malt04-10-07.

As you will see from my CV, although I am relatively young, I have already got basic experience in jobs related to the hotel sector. In particular, I would like to point out the front office experience I gained through my work placement in a hotel reception in Lugo, the city where I study. I also did a three-month summer job in France, where I worked with adults and teenagers as an entertainer. Because of this, I think that my communication and organizational skills are good.

My mother tongue is Spanish, but I have been studying English for ten years now, first at secondary school, and now at the *Escuela Universitaria de Turismo*, where I am in my final year. I am confident that I can carry out all my duties in English, and I also speak good French.

I am a positive, energetic person with an open nature. I enjoy being with clients and holidaymakers, and I think it is fair to say that I am hard-working and adaptable. I have been abroad several times, so I am not worried about working and living abroad. I regularly go walking, and I enjoy sports activities in general.

I am available for interview at any time after February 25.

Yours sincerely

Marta Elena Gutiérrez Alvarez

CV Post your CV at www.myCV.com and enable the *Hotelwork4U* option. Your CV will then be sent to us automatically when you press the Apply Online button below.

Job details

Job: Hotel entertainer

Location: Corfu – Greece

Description: Hotel entertainment work in Greece between April and October. Working with kids, helping hotel guests to have fun, organizing the sports and activities programme … Are you a hard worker? Then we are waiting for you and will train you before you start with TopAnimation.

Salary: €450 – €750 / month depending on experience.

Skills Required:

Language requirements:

English – Very good   Any other languages
French – Good   an advantage
German – Good

Aerobic or sports instructor skills a real advantage. Proven ability to work with kids

Education required: Minimum = GCSE 'A' level or local equivalent. Tourism qualification preferable.

Experience required: None essential, but all relevant experience an advantage.

MARTA ELENA GUTIÉRREZ ALVAREZ

Term address (until 30/06/20–) **1**
Avda Ramón y Cajal, 53, 6A
27011, Lugo, Spain

Tel (+34) 663 246 357

Nationality Spanish (EU citizen) **2**

Home address
Santa Rufino, 12, 3B
33396, Gijón, Spain

Email margutal@hotmail.com

Final year tourism management student with good IT, organizational, and customer skills, seeking a front office career with an international hotel group. **3**

EDUCATION

2005–2008	**Escuela Universitaria De Turismo** **4** **, Lugo, Spain** Diploma en Turismo (Equivalent to UK HND Tourism Management) **5** Expected grade: Pass with merit **6**
2003–2005	**I.E.S Cienfuego** **7** Bachillerato (Equivalent to UK GCSE 'A'-level). Grade: 7,2

PROFESSIONAL EXPERIENCE

Summer 2004	**Résidence Les Dunes du Médoc, Soulac, France** Entertainment work with adults and teenagers. Occasionally did reception duties. Learned to deal with face-to-face customer situations. **8**
December 2003	**Hotel La Muralla Romana, Lugo, Spain** Work placement. Reception duties including taking telephone reservations, check-in, check-out, and group bookings.
Summer 2003	**Viajes Atenas, Gijón, Spain** Travel agency sales and ticketing and holiday sales. Developed basic sales technique and customer care skills.

SKILLS

IT	**Savia-Amadeus** – course in IT skills for travel agency sales & ticketing **9** Microsoft Office – competent in Word, Excel, and PowerPoint.
Languages	Spanish – native language English – upper-intermediate written and spoken. Cambridge ESOL CAE. **10** French – upper-intermediate spoken.

INTERESTS **11**

Travel	I enjoy discovering new places and cultures. I have travelled widely in Spain. I have been to the UK twice and to France.
Sport	Mountaineering

REFERENCES

(Email correspondence in English welcome) **12**

The Principal
E. U. de Turismo, Lugo

Email: escuela@
escueturlug.com

The Manager
Résidence Les Dunes du Médoc, Soulac du Mer

Email: mérignacp@les
dunesdumedoc.fr

---

1 If you live away from home, give both your term-time and your permanent address.

2 Your nationality will help to clarify your work permit status. You are not obliged to give other personal details such as age or marital status.

3 Offer a short profile of yourself. Use positive language and say what you are looking for.

4 Do not translate the names of places, companies, or institutions into English.

5 Do not translate qualifications into English. Give an equivalent if this is appropriate.

6 If you are still studying, give grades so far, or an expected final grade.

7 Give education details from most recent to least.

8 Give details of the duties and responsibilities you had in jobs or work placement.

9 Indicate the skills and knowledge you gained on courses you followed.

10 Indicate any second language qualifications you have.

11 Your interests tell your employer what type of person you are. People who travel are often adventurous and independent.

12 Offer two references – an academic one from your centre of study and a professional reference from work placement or a previous job.

5 Reporting incidents

Incidents that happen to tourists on holiday with your company or in your hotel must be reported in the incident log.

1 Think of three typical incidents that can happen to a tourist during a package holiday. Tell your partner what they are. Did you think of the same incidents?

2 Look at the page from the log for the Hotel Ozukara in Turkey.

1 What had happened to the guests affected by the incident?

2 When and where did the incident take place?

3 How many people did the incident involve?

4 What action was taken to solve the problem?

5 Who reported the incident for the tour operator?

6 Whose fault was the incident?

3 Look at the notes from an incident at the Red Sea Paradise hotel. Use the notes to prepare an entry in an incident log like the one from **2**.

Turkish Meditour   Incident log

Resort: Bodrum
Hotel : *Ozukara (3-star)*
Incident reported by: *Jacqueline Dakota*
Type of incident: *Overbooking*

Sheet no. TM Bod-0803-10
Post: *Transfer rep*
Date of incident: *15th July*

Details of incident:

On arrival at the hotel with Group ozu-071508, I went to the hotel reception to book the group in. The hotel arrivals list and the transfer list did not coincide. Three couples (the Coopers, the Fergusons, & the McKittericks) were without rooms. Two clients (Mr Copperthwaite & Mr Spencer) had been put into a twin despite having paid the supplement for single rooms.

The hotel offered alternative rooms in the company's 4-star Kassandra, a sister hotel, 5 km further south. Two couples (the Coopers & the Fergusons) accepted this, but the McKittericks refused. They claimed that the alternative hotel was too far from Bodrum. Both single-room clients requested upgrading to the Kassandra.

After a brief negotiation, I opted to put Mr Copperthwaite & Mr Spencer into the Kassandra and gave the room that had been freed to the McKittericks, who accepted it.

The next morning the hotel staff and I compared registration lists. We had failed to update our list. The hotel had responded correctly to the list we had initially sent.

Signed
J Dakota

16th July, 20—

Resort – Elphistone
Hotel – Red Sea Paradise
Date of incident – 27th August
Type – damage to guests' personal effects
Clients – Mr Bob Moorland & Mrs Freda Moorland

Guests arrived with group – all normal. Group registration done without problems & guests all went up to allocated rooms. 20 mins. later Moorlands rang office & asked me to go to room. Once in room, they showed me suitcase with evident damage – handle broken, lock also. Moorlands explained had been obliged to break lock to access suitcase. Insisted that case OK at airport. Claimed damage done in transfer.

Am unable to demonstrate that Moorlands' case was in perfect condition at airport, so opted to accept responsibility for damage. Offered to get damage repaired at resort. Moorlands refused offer & requested new case once back in UK. Have accepted and will file incident thru' standard company insurance.

Writing bank key

1 Report writing

1 1 Rahel de Jong and Christian Koller
  2 Managers of local TIC and other tourism decision-makers
  3 from internet search engines such as Google and Yahoo (key words: Dublin tourist information multimedia), the Tourist Offices Worldwide Directory (www.towd.com), and visits to local TICs
  4 positive: excellent, good, attractive, comprehensive, effective, useful
  5 interactive and multimedia facilities at the Dublin Tourist Office
  6 (Possible answers) (a) podcasts, video, webcam; (b) e-cards, screensavers, webcam

2 1 Facilities at the TIC
  2 Mode of presentation
  3 Methodology
  4 Follow-up work

3 1 Information was collected from various sources.
  2 The following sources were particularly useful in compiling this report.
  3 Tourist Information Centres in the city do not appear to be so well presented or accessible.
  4 Text in all these sections was comprehensive without being too long.
  5 Prepare proposals for how some of the Dublin features might be included in our own regional tourist information services.

4 Past Simple (Note: Present Simple and Present Perfect also occur)
  Active: were particularly useful, was visually very attractive, it was very easy to …, there were links to …, we particularly liked …, which gave details of …
  Passive: Information was collected from …, was then selected and ordered, was found

2 Information leaflet

1 1 25 minutes
  2 Star Ferry Terminal Building
  3 Dim sum
  4 Temple Street and Ladies' Market in Mong Kok
  5 Victoria Peak
  6 Opia in the Jia Hotel
  7 daily 8.00 a.m. to 6.00 p.m.

2 1 48 HOURS IN HONG KONG. Yes, 48 hours = a weekend.
  2 Discover the delights of China's most exciting city in a weekend. More 'promotional'.
  3 Getting there, Get your bearings, Check in, Take a walk, Lunch on the run, Window shopping, Take a view, Dinner with the locals, Sunday morning: go to the temple. Yes, easy to see. Yes, they indicate the content.
  4 phone numbers and websites

3 Possible answers
  1 Cathay Pacific, Qantas … fly non-stop to Hong Kong
  Both parts have modern hotels …
  Accommodation in Hong Kong can be expensive.
  The trek ends in the little fishing village of Shek O.
  Dim sum is a Chinese institution.
  Modern shopping malls are all over the city.
  The Peak Tram … makes a near vertical climb …
  Most locals head for the buzzing restaurants …
  A good place to feel the religious atmosphere and breathe in the incense smoke is Man Mo Temple
  2 Accommodation in Hong Kong can be expensive.
  The Hong Kong Tourism Office in the Star Ferry Terminal Building can help with other options.
  The customers are mostly Chinese and you can watch the old women playing mah-jong.
  3 Discover the delights of China's most exciting city in a weekend.
  Head to the hills.
  Take the bus back to the city centre.

3 Public notices

1 The weather is going to get very stormy.

2 Some were going on a boat trip and others were going to climb the Teide mountain.

3 Go shopping and sightseeing in Puerto de la Cruz.

4 He forgot to warn people to prepare their tents for the high winds.

5 B. It is more formal. It uses complete sentences. It asks readers to sign a list or contact the office. It is signed by the campsite rep in name of the company.

4 Email job application

1 4, 5, 7, 8

2 She begins with a reference to the job she is seeking. She ends by saying when she is available for interview.

3 1 Lugo
  2 Gijón
  3 Skills – foreign language and IT skills (Savia-Amadeus and MS Office). Job experience – reception duties in hotels in Lugo and Soulac.
  4 Because this is the accepted way to organize them in CVs

4 She has begun with her professional experience in hotel reception work. She has highlighted her language skills. She has given a description of her personality.

5 Reporting incidents

1 Lost documents (passport, air tickets, etc). Client falls ill, is injured, or becomes sunburnt. Client involved in an accident. Complaints about room, food, or other services. Client fails to show up for a trip.

2 1 When they arrived at their hotel, there were no rooms for them.
  2 15th July. The Hotel Ozukara, Bodrum.
  3 8: 3 couples, Mr Copperthwaite, and Mr Spencer
  4 2 couples, Mr Copperthwaite, and Mr Spencer were sent to the 4-star Kassandra. The McKittericks were given a double room in the Ozukara.
  5 J Dakota
  6 Turkish Meditour, the tour operator. They had not given the hotel the latest registration list.

7 Attractions and events

Take off

1 What are these places? Are there similar visitor attractions in your country?

2 Work in pairs. Say the name of a country or a city to your partner. Your partner must think of a visitor attraction there.

3 Take turns to say the names of different countries or cities, until you have each got ten places plus attractions.

Vocabulary

Types of visitor attractions

1 What are the most popular visitor attractions in your city or region?

2 Which of the categories in the table do they belong to?

3 Can you think of another example for each of the types of attraction?

4 Explain the difference between the following pairs of words.

1 lake / river	5 festival / parade
2 mountain / hill	6 nightclub / casino
3 museum / art gallery	7 theme park / national park
4 palace / castle	8 theatre / concert hall

Natural	Built	
• mountains (e.g. the Himalayas) • lakes and rivers • national park (e.g. Yosemite, USA) • heritage coast	• historic site (e.g. Shakespeare's birthplace, Stratford-upon-Avon, UK) • archaelogical site (e.g. Forum, Rome, Italy) • monument (e.g. Nelson's Column, Trafalgar Square, London)	• museum • art gallery (e.g. Louvre, Paris) • theme park (e.g. Disneyland) • palace / stately home (e.g. Versailles, France) • castle
Events	**Entertainment and leisure**	
• music / arts festival (e.g. Edinburgh Festival, UK) • religious festival • carnival (e.g. Rio de Janeiro, Brazil) • parade (e.g. Gay Pride, San Francisco)	• theatre • concert hall • nightclub • casino • zoo	• shopping • sports centre / stadium (e.g. Wembley, London)

In this unit
- types of visitor attractions
- describing built attractions
- describing festivals and events
- people and facilities at attractions
- bringing attractions to life

Pronunciation

1 🎧 Listen to the sounds underlined in the words below. Which sound do you hear? Tick (✓) the right column.

	say /eɪ/	no /əʊ/	hear /ɪə/
1 coast			
2 home			
3 lake			
4 parade			
5 Rome			
6 Shakespeare			
7 Shakespeare			
8 stadium			
9 stately			
10 theatre			

2 The sounds underlined are diphthongs – two vowels close together in the same syllable. They are long sounds. The first part is stressed more than the second.

Practise saying the words one column at a time. Pay attention to the length of the sound underlined. Remember to stress the first part of the sound most.

3 Go to the *Key words* for Units 1 – 6. Find words that contain the diphthong sounds.

Reading

Trends in visitor attractions

1 What changes have there been in the four categories of attractions in the last thirty years? Think about when your parents were the age that you are now.

2 Read the article. Did you identify any of the changes mentioned? What other trends are described?

3 Find at least one example of each of the four categories of types of visitor attraction.

4 Find examples of particular ways in which attractions are made more interesting and exciting.

Inside tourism: the changing face of the 'attractions industry'

As the wishes and tastes of tourists and visitors change, tourist attractions have to change as well. In the last twenty or thirty years, there have been some significant developments.

Natural attractions like sandy beaches and mountains cannot change very much, but nevertheless there have been developments, in particular a concern to preserve the environment and to make any buildings fit into the natural context.

Perhaps the greatest changes have been in man-made attractions like museums and historic sites, which have become more interesting and entertaining places to visit, while still maintaining their role of teaching visitors about the past. In many of them, the aim is not just to display the past, but to take visitors into the past in an interactive way. Some have been converted into 'living museums' where actors in costumes meet the public and play the roles of characters from the past. In others, history is made vivid and exciting through the use of realistic waxworks, animatronic models, sounds, and even smells, to conjure up a sense of the past.

Traditional festivals by definition do not change very much, but there has been a trend to increase the number of special events and festivals as cities realise that holding a music festival or an arts event is a good way of attracting tourists.

Entertainment and leisure facilities are always having to change. In the developed world, the simple rectangular swimming pool, for example, is no longer enough – it has to be a water park, with flumes, chutes, splash zones, and wave machines.

The tourist is always looking for new attractions, and the 'attractions industry' has to keep on changing.

Vocabulary

Architectural features

1 Match the pictures of architectural features with the glossary of terms.

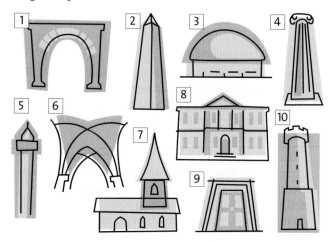

Glossary

arch curved structure with straight sides, often supporting a bridge or the roof of a large building

column tall, solid vertical post made of stone, supporting or decorating a building or standing alone

dome round roof on a building

façade the front wall of a large building that you see from the outside

minaret tall, thin tower, usually forming part of a mosque

obelisk a tall pointed stone column with four sides, put up in memory of a person or an event

portal a large impressive door or entrance

spire tall, pointed tower on the top of a church

tower tall, narrow building, or part of a building, either square or round

vaulted ceiling decorated roof made from a series of arches joined together

2 In which type of building would you find them (e.g. *cathedral, mosque*)?

3 Can you think of any famous buildings that have these features?

4 Add one of these words to the word groups listed below.

construct	granite	statue
long	show	alongside

1 high, wide, thick, _____

2 underneath, in front of, _____

3 depict, represent, _____

4 build, erect, _____

5 marble, stone, _____

6 carving, sculpture, _____

Reading

Two top Paris attractions

Read the descriptions of two famous buildings in Paris. Each description has four sections. Which section

1 describes the use and function of the building?

2 describes when and why it was built?

3 gives some detailed description?

4 gives a general physical description?

Arc de Triomphe

a The Arc de Triomphe was erected in the early 19th century as a tribute to the French army of Napoleon. It is built of marble.

b The arch is over 50 metres high, 45 metres wide, and 22 metres thick.

c There are four sculptures carved on the façade. The most famous is *La Marseillaise*. It depicts the departure of the volunteers encouraged by a winged figure representing France.

d The arch is used for special processions. Underneath the arch is the Tomb of the Unknown Soldier. A flame is lit every evening at 6.30 p.m.

Notre-Dame cathedral

a The cathedral of Notre-Dame was started by Bishop de Sully in 1163 and work continued for nearly 200 years. It was completed in 1345. The cathedral is dedicated to the Virgin Mary and stands in the centre of Paris on the Ile-de-la-Cité.

b It is undoubtedly the finest example of French gothic architecture. The twin towers are a famous feature of the Paris skyline, and are 69 metres high. The spire, which was added in the 19th century, is 90 metres high.

c The façade is the most striking part of the building. The three portals are adorned with remarkable stone sculptures, including the Last Judgement. The rose window in the façade was built over 700 years ago and is magnificent.

d The cathedral is still used for regular church services as well as special occasions. The vast interior can accommodate 9,000 people. French road distances are established from the '0 km' point located on the square in front of the cathedral entrance.

● Language spot

The Passive

1 Find a form of these verbs in the descriptions in *Reading*.

1 erect	4 use	7 continue	10 establish
2 build	5 light	8 stand	
3 depict	6 start	9 adorn	

a Which are Present tenses and which are Past tenses?

b Which are Passive and which are Active?

c Find other examples of Passive and Active verbs.

2 Is the Passive used more than the Active because

1 descriptions like this are more formal?

2 we are thinking about what *is done* to the thing we are interested in, not about what it *does*?

3 sometimes we don't know *who* or *what* does the action (i.e. who is the 'agent')?

4 it makes the text more interesting?

3 Which preposition (*by*, *of*, *for*) is used to describe

1 the person (or thing) who did it?

2 the reason or function?

3 the material used?

4 Write descriptions using these notes.

a **Nelson's Column, London**
- *In Trafalgar Square – constructed 1829–1841 – commemorate Battle of Trafalgar 1805*
- *Column = 56 m; statue of Nelson 5.5 m. Granite*
- *Base: 4 giant bronze lions (sculptor = Landseer) – represent strength of British Empire*
- *A place to meet – celebrating New Year*

b **Buckingham Palace, London**
- *Originally a country house for Duke of Buckingham – converted to palace 1825 (architect = Nash)*
- *Official royal residence 1837–present*
- *Façade redesigned 1913 – 429 rooms (78 bathrooms) – employs 335 staff*
- *Buckingham Palace open to public August and September. Also art gallery*

>> Go to **Grammar reference** p.122

lagoon (n) a lake of salt water that is separated from the sea by a reef or an area of rock or sand

mass (n) a ceremony held in memory of the last meal that Christ had with his disciples

plague (n) an infectious disease that kills a lot of people

redeemer (n) Jesus Christ

Listening

Describing a festival

1 🎧 Listen to a guide describing the Festa del Redentore in Venice. As you listen, follow the written text and indicate places where the guide

   1 adds something that is not in the text [↑],

   2 misses out, changes, or uses different words [__].
   The first paragraph is done for you as an example.

2 Go to p.113 and check your answers.

3 🎧 Listen again. Complete the key expressions used by the guide.

   1 Good morning, _____. Welcome to Venice.

   2 My name is Carlotta and I _____ your guide for this weekend.

   3 Before I start, can _____ me at the back?

   4 Let me start _____ a little about the history of the festival.

   5 From 1575 to 77, as _____, Venice was …

   6 Now, _____ the festival itself. What _____ is this:

   7 By _____, if you're wondering about …

   8 The climax of the festival and the most significant part if you remember _____ about the history of the festival, is …

   9 Oh, one thing I _____ is that …

   10 So, that's the Festa del Redentore. As _____, it's a wonderful event.

   11 Are there _____?

Festa del Redentore

Location	Venice, Italy
Timing	third weekend of July
Duration	two days
Information	www.comune.venezia. it/turismo

Introduction

↑ The Festa del Redentore – the Festival of the **Redeemer** – is a high point of the Venice summer. Thanks to a spectacular firework display, the Redentore is a major tourist attraction.

History

From 1575–77, Venice was hit by a terrible **plague** which killed more than a third of the city's inhabitants. In 1576, the city's leader, the Doge, promised to erect a church dedicated to the Redeemer, in return for help in ending the plague. On July 13, 1577, the plague was declared over, and work began to construct the church. It was also decided that Venice would forever give thanks on the third Sunday of July.

4 Look at the comparison between the characteristics of written and spoken descriptions.

Written	Spoken
Use of headings and paragraphs	Introductory phrases (e.g. *Let me start by telling you about …*)
Longer sentences	Shorter sentences; sentence breaks
Passive forms	Passive is used, but not so frequently – instead use of 'you' (e.g. *You can make arrangements …*)
No interaction with the reader	Interaction with the audience (e.g. *Can you all hear me at the back?*)
Punctuation (e.g. brackets)	Pauses, linking phrases (e.g. *By the way …*)

5 Find examples of each characteristic (written and spoken) in the text and script about the Festa del Redentore.

Festivals and events are among the most successful tools available to communities, cities, states, regions, and countries to increase tourism, create powerful and memorable branding and imaging opportunities, encourage positive media coverage, effect economic impact, and enhance the quality of life for those who live there.
IFEA
(International Festivals and Events Association) www.ifea.com

What happens

From early on the Saturday, boats are decorated with flowers, lanterns, and balloons. St Mark's **lagoon** fills with as many as two thousand boats, their occupants eating and drinking as they wait for the traditional spectacular display of fireworks. (Arrangements can easily be made through your hotel for an evening with dinner on a boat.) At around 11.30 p.m., the display begins and the lagoon becomes one of the most atmospheric stages in the world, fireworks illuminating the spires, domes, and bell towers of the city.

On Sunday, a pontoon of decorated gondolas and other boats is strung across the Giudecca canal to allow the faithful to walk to the church of the Redentore. The climax of the festival is the **mass** held in the presence of the Patriarch of Venice, a reminder that the Festa has a serious side.

For more information, visit the website quoted above.

Writing

Three festivals

1 Work in groups of three. Student A, go to p.111. Student B, go to p.112. Student C, go to p.117. Write a description of your festival from the notes.

2 When you have finished, look at each other's descriptions and suggest any corrections or improvements.

3 In your groups, think of two festivals (or ceremonies or parades) from your country. Write a description of them.

Customer care
Different cultures, different responses

1 How can the people who work at tourist attractions adapt to meet the cultural differences of certain nationalities, for example, Japan or the Middle East?

2 Read the case study to find out what one tourist attraction has done.

> **Case study: Japanese visitors to the home of Beatrix Potter in north-west England.**
> Beatrix Potter, who wrote children's books about characters such as Peter Rabbit and Jemima Puddleduck, is very popular in Japan, especially since the release of the film *Miss Potter* in 2007. Her home, Hill Top Cottage, is now owned by the National Trust and Japanese tourists make up a third of all visitors. The local tourist industry prepares tourism employees in a number of ways.

Japanese culture	Tourist industry response
Courtesy and politeness are very important in Japanese culture.	Special courtesy training programmes, including teaching the correct pronunciation of *yokoso*, the Japanese word for 'welcome'.
Japanese people usually greet by bowing.	Staff are being taught how to bow with the correct amount of formality.
Giving and receiving little gifts is very important in Japanese culture.	The gift shop stocks items that Japanese like to buy, and packages each one in a separate National Trust bag so they can be given as individual gifts.

The Golden Gate National Parks Conservancy is a non-profit membership organization created to preserve the Golden Gate National Parks, enhance the experiences of park visitors, and build a community dedicated to conserving the parks for the future.

from the Golden Gate National Parks Conservancy (which manages Alcatraz and other national parklands in the Bay Area) mission statement
www.parksconservancy.org

Vocabulary

People and facilities at attractions

1 Match these descriptions of people who work at attractions and things you find at attractions in A with the words in B.

A	B
People	a activity sheet
1 shows tourists or travellers where to go	b animatronics
2 looks after a forest or park	c audio-tour
3 looks after things that are kept in a museum	d curator
4 translates what someone has said into another language	e guide
5 supervises and rescues people who are in difficulty in the water (at a beach or swimming pool)	f interpreter
6 protects a building	g lifeguard
	h period costume
Things	i ranger
7 the art of moving a lifelike figure or person by electronic means	j re-enactment
8 a written board that gives directions and distances	k role-play
9 repeating the actions of a past event	l security guard
10 activity in which you take the part of someone else	m signpost
11 exhibition of models of people (not moving)	n waxworks
12 piece of paper to write down answers to questions as you visit an attraction	
13 clothes from the past	
14 recorded description of an attraction	

2 At which attractions would you expect to find these people and things?

Where in the world?

Read about Alcatraz in San Francisco.

1 What different functions has Alcatraz had in its history?

2 Why do tourists go there?

3 Who can you listen to on the audio-tour?

Alcatraz

'You are entitled to food, clothing, shelter, and medical attention. Anything else you get is a privilege.'
(Alcatraz Prison Rules and Regulations no. 5, 1934)

This rule was one of the realities of life inside the walls of the US Federal Penitentiary, Alcatraz Island. The subject of many movies and books, Alcatraz has become a symbol of America's dark side. From fiction rather than fact, we have stories of the prison and some of the men who lived in its cells – Al 'Scarface' Capone and Robert Stroud, the 'Birdman of Alcatraz', for example. The truth of Alacatraz has often been overlooked, lost in the fog of its myths.

Form your own opinions, and explore the island's mysteries. For it does indeed have a mysterious presence, one shaded by the uses to which society has put it. This island in the heart of San Francisco Bay, just two kilometres from the sights and sounds of one of the world's most beautiful cities, has been used as a fort, a lighthouse, and a prison. Today, it is a Golden Gate National Recreation Area, and the National Park Service is working to make it accessible to visitors, preserve its buildings, protect its birds and other wildlife, and interpret its history.

Take the cell house audio-tour and hear some of the officers and inmates talking about their experience on 'The Rock'.

www.nps.gov/alcatraz

Find out

Choose four attractions from your country from the list you made in *Vocabulary* on p.60. Try to include one from each of the categories. Find out more about each one and complete the table. In the final row, include your personal opinion of how exciting and entertaining the attraction is.

Attraction				
Description				
Website				
Changes in last 20 / 30 years				
Opening hours / visitor information				
Excitement / entertainment rating (0 to 5)				

Key words

Nouns
activity sheet
animatronics
arch
audio-tour
column
dome
façade
marble
monument
national park
parade
period costume
procession
ranger
re-enactment
sculpture
waxworks

Adjective
dedicated to

Verbs
construct
depict
erect
represent

Speaking

Bringing attractions to life

Work in groups.

1 Choose the two visitor attractions from *Find out* which had the lowest excitement / entertainment rating. Decide how they could be made more exciting and entertaining, and 'brought alive' – for example, by using actors, animatronics, waxworks, audio-tours, and so on.

2 Show your ideas to another group.

Next stop

1 Have you ever been on a coach tour or guided tour that you have either really enjoyed or really disliked? Where was it? What did you see?

2 What made the tour successful / unsuccessful?

3 What problems do you think can occur on a guided tour, either on a coach or another form of transport?

8 On tour

Take off

1 What do you know about the three places in the pictures?

2 Can you find them on a map of the world?

3 Why do you think tourists would visit them? What types of tours might they go on – for example, *cruises, walking tours, museum visits*?

Reading

Three tours

1 Read about the three tours. In groups, discuss the questions.

Which of the tours involve

1 a private performance?
2 visiting ancient ruins?
3 travelling on a boat?
4 accommodation in the city centre?
5 seeing rare animals in their natural habitat?
6 an internal flight?
7 talks by an expert?

Libya

Ecuador

St Petersburg

a Libya – Lost cities of the Greek and Roman Empires

- Starting from Tripoli, ancient city and capital of Libya. Nearby is Leptis, probably the best preserved Roman city in the Mediterranean world.

- Fly east to the less often visited region of Cyrenaica, a land of beautiful green hills running down to the crystal turquoise waters of the Mediterranean.

- Discover the ancient port of Apollonia, an enchanting city now partly sunk beneath the sea which forms a dazzling backdrop to its theatre and the columns of its Byzantine churches.

- Visit the city of Cyrene, founded in the 7th century BC and for centuries the most important Greek city in North Africa – its stunning temple of Zeus is larger than the Parthenon in Athens.

- Extra tour to the Sahara Desert.

b Ecology of Ecuador – The enchanted islands of the Galapagos

- A special tour accompanied by guest lecturer, Dr Michael Brooke, Curator of Birds, Cambridge University Museum of Zoology.

- Travel in a specially modified cruiser, adapted for the Galapagos. All cabins are air-conditioned outside cabins with private toilet / shower room.

- The tour begins with a visit to colonial Quito, plus a tour of the Avenue of Volcanoes, among stunning scenery.

- The South American archipelago of the Galapagos Islands is home to an amazing variety of wildlife – giant tortoises, marine iguanas, and many more.

- Optional tour of the Ecuadorian Amazon – a journey to another world.

In this unit
- the job of tour manager / tour guide
- standards of performance
- arrangements on tour
- giving a commentary and telling stories
- problems on tour

2 Match these notes written by the tour operator with the correct tour. In each case, decide what the notes mean.

1 ⬛ ▬ ▭ ✕
> Book local guide for city panoramic tour.
> Lecture in museum – English language?
> Hotel facilities
> Double-check availability of HB

2
Airport arrival - meet and greet?
Book coach transfers (plus local guide)
Local guides at various sights?
Check accommodation arrangements for the
Sahara tour - tents?

3 ⬛ ▬ ▭ ✕
> Check first-class cabin for guest lecturer.
> Staff on cruiser – English-speaking?
> Local guide for tour of volcanoes.
> Land-based travel? Jeeps?

[c] St Petersburg – City of music

- Tour to one of the world's most magical cities, including a number of concerts in grand settings (e.g. Sheremetev Palace, where students of the St Petersburg Music Conservatory will perform works by Tchaikovsky exclusively for our group).
- Programme covers all the principle sights of Peter the Great's magnificent city, from the Hermitage, with its priceless Scythian gold collection, to the Catherine Palace at Pushkin, with its recently-restored Amber Room.
- We will also have the services of Humphrey Burton, one of Britain's most distinguished television directors and commentators to help bring out the musical magic.
- We stay throughout at the Dostoyevsky Hotel in the heart of St Petersburg.

3 Which tourism professionals will be employed on the tours?

EXAMPLE
a guide at the museum

4 Which tour would you most like to work on? What job would you like to do on the tour? Why?

Listening

From tour guide to tour manager

1 🎧 Tourism trainees do not usually find a job as tour manager as their first job. Listen to Gina Meadows describe what she did before she became a tour manager. Note down the training she did and any jobs she had.

2 🎧 Listen again and write T (true) or F (false).
1 Gina always wanted to work in tourism.
2 The qualification she got is recognized in many European countries.
3 She got the job she wanted immediately.
4 Her experience of travelling was more important than the qualification.
5 She spent two years working as a tour guide before becoming a tour manager.
6 She likes her job.

A guide takes on a number of roles for the tourist: teacher, entertainer, ambassador, nurse, and 'the boss'.
Jenny Townsend
London Blue Badge Tourist Guide

It's my job

Read about Lucy Tovchikh from Ukraine.

1 What does Lucy like / dislike about her job?
2 How does she try to make her tours interesting?
3 What other job does she do?
4 Which of her special tours would you choose to go on?

Find out

What job opportunities are there for tour guides in your area (on coach tours, cruise ships, or at visitor attractions)?

What qualifications and experience do the companies require?

What training do they give – for example, on giving commentaries and presentations, health and safety, dealing with problems?

Ludmila (Lucy) Tovchikh

How long have you been working as a tour guide?
For more than ten years.

What does your job involve?
Researching, exploring, reading, designing a tour, guiding. For me, it's always important to know who I will guide for beforehand – what country tourists are from, their ages, their reason for visiting Odessa. It helps me to evaluate their background knowledge and to provide a tour in a certain way.

What are the main sights and attractions in your city?
The beautiful Opera House built by Viennese architects at the end of the nineteenth century.

The Potyomkin Steps connected with the mutiny on the battleship 'Prince Potyomkin' in 1905 and a famous film by Eisenstein.

The non-stop beach nightlife with lots of discos, restaurants, and bars.

Do you do any special tours?
Yes, I do *Criminals of Odessa, Catacombs, Jewish Odessa, Palaces of Odessa*, and a very special tour which only I do – *Pirates of Odessa*, which involves changing into pirate costumes, visiting a pirates' cave, and listening to and singing pirate songs.

What do you enjoy most about your job?
I try to make a sort of performance for my tourists. I hate boring academic tours with lots of dates in them. People usually forget them. They remember the impression about the city. Some interesting stories. Sometimes I even dance and sing.

What do you find most challenging?
Big groups of people and a stressful schedule. It happens when I work for a cruise ship.

Have you had any interesting people on your tours?
What do you mean by 'interesting'? If you mean famous, yes. I did tours for some famous Russian actors, composers, and writers. If you mean nice to talk to, sure. Almost all of them were interesting. I always learn something from people I guide for.

Apart from guiding, do you do any other work?
Yes, I teach English. That's also a sort of performance.

Do you have any particular plans for the future?
Apart from guiding, I love travelling. Next year I'm going to Siberia to see Lake Baikal with my Dutch friend and then for a cycling tour around Holland.

Any advice for someone about to start as a Tour Guide?
Love what you are doing. Be inquisitive and enthusiastic.

Vocabulary

Standards of performance

1 Use the words and phrases below to complete the 'Standards of performance' advice sheet to tour guides from a training manual.

anecdotes	first-aid kit	rapport
body language	gestures	seat belts
clarity	hazards	sense of humour
eye contact	microphone	tone

STANDARDS of PERFORMANCE

Aim: To inform, entertain, and care for visitors, and enhance their experience

- Establish a welcoming _____ [1] with the group by smiling when you greet the group and introducing yourself and the driver.

- Use open _body language_ [2] – do not fold arms, do not keep hands in pockets.

- Control hand and arm _____ [3].

- Check that the _microphone_ [4] is switched on and working, and adjust it to ensure _clarity_ [5].

- Make sure that you are looking at everyone and establish _eye contact_ [6] when talking to the group.

- Use voice correctly with a variety of pitch and a lively _tone_ [7].

- Be enthusiastic and use your _sense of humore_ [8] to entertain and make the group smile and laugh when appropriate.

- Tell stories and _anecdotes_ [9], but try not to make them too long.

- Inform group about safety, use of _____ [10] on the coach, _seat belts_ [11], and emergency procedures.

- Warn group of _hazards_ [12], e.g. while walking and getting off the coach.

2 What do you think these technical abbreviations and terms used by tour managers / guides mean?

1 comfort break
2 grats
3 Must Tells
4 panoramic
5 pax
6 rooming list
7 Top Visual Priorities

Customer care

Personal appearance

How important is the way you dress and your personal appearance in tourism? Read this extract from the 'Standards of performance' for a national Tour Guide Association.

1 How would the standards be different for (a) a hot country, (b) a Muslim country, (c) your country?

2 Change the standards so that they are appropriate for your country.

Dress appropriately for the occasion

- city guiding – tailored trousers or skirt and a jacket for women, tailored trousers for men with jacket and tie
- country or island guiding – as for city, but jackets may be replaced by smart sweater
- weatherproof clothing and footwear, depending on season
- outdoor activities – appropriate protective clothing for weather and conditions
- be aware of personal hygiene and condition of clothing

What is it?

Listening

Practicalities on tour

1 At which stage of a tour would you expect to hear the expressions listed below? Write your answers under 'Exercise 1' in the table.

1 when checking arrangements with other tourism service providers (e.g. hotel)
2 when talking to passengers at the start of the tour
3 when talking to passengers during the trip
4 when talking to Head Office (tour operator)
5 when talking to passengers when getting off the coach

	Exercise 1	Exercise 2
a If you look to your left in a moment, you'll see …	3	C
b Hi, this is Sarah, the guide from Galloway Tours.	2	A
c Please be back on the coach in thirty minutes' time.	5 ✓	E
d Can you all hear me OK?	2 or 3	B
e If that's a problem, call me back on the mobile.	4	D
f Is the temperature OK?	2	B
g While I've got you, can I just check something else?	1, 4	A
h We're going to take a break here.	3, 5	E
i For the moment, just sit back and relax.	2	B
j Hi, this is Sarah again. There's another problem.	4	D
k So I'll tell you something about …	3, 2	C
l I'm just checking you got my message.	4, 1	A
m Your driver today is Ken.	2	B
n Please be careful as you get off.	5	E

Toilet (BE)
washroom / bathroom / restroom (NAE)

2 🎧 Listen to the extracts from five conversations or commentaries – they correspond with situations 1 to 5 in **1**. Write the letter of the conversation in the last column.

● Language spot

Explaining arrangements

1 What are the different tenses used in these sentences? Choose from the following.

1 Present Simple   4 Future Continuous
2 Present Continuous   5 *going to* future
3 *will* future

a You're not getting in until 9.00 p.m.
b I'll be looking after you today.
c We're going to be on the coach quite a lot today.
d We're taking a scenic route through the countryside.
e We will be stopping for lunch in a very nice hilltop restaurant.
f I'll be telling you a little bit about the countryside.
g I'll tell you something about this traditional dress.
h We're going to have to take a two-hour break.
i We're going to take a break here.
j The coach departs at 11.05 precisely.
k There'll be a lot of coaches parked here.

2 All the sentences in **1** describe the future. Which forms are used to describe

1 a timetabled arrangement?
2 a definite arrangement?
3 a future action over a period of time, or an action that will happen as part of a schedule?
4 an intention?
5 a decision to do something not pre-arranged?

3 Put the verbs in brackets in the correct tense.

1 You say there are two extra for dinner? In that case, we _____ (set) an extra table.
2 We need to be at the station at 11.30 tomorrow because the train _____ (leave) at 11.45.
3 We _____ (stop) in a few minutes so that you can take some photos.
4 We _____ (arrive) in Edinburgh at 5.00 p.m.
5 Later on I _____ (give out) questionnaires for you to fill in.

» Go to **Grammar reference** p.123

Speaking

Checking the schedule

Role-play the conversations between a tour guide and a hotel, and a tour guide and a driver. Student A, go to p.109. Student B, go to p.114.

Writing

Preparing notes for commentaries

1 Work in groups of four. Read sections b and e of the commentary on p.133 and identify what the speakers actually say for these notes.

Things to remember at start

welcome
check microphone
introduce self and driver
comfortable?
temperature?
explain day – lunch, visit
    castle, arrive hotel
    6.00 p.m.
relax – commentary later

Getting off reminders

thank you – enjoy?
break – coffee and
toilets
back in 30 minutes
    (check time)
be careful (steep steps)

2 Work in pairs. You are guides. Choose either A or B below and say what the guide would actually say for these notes. Your partner should compare your commentary with the text on p.116.

A | TOP VISUAL PRIORITY: **DESCRIPTION**

TOWER BRIDGE

Before bridge – one of most famous sights
Tower Bridge – started 1886 – took 8 years
great engineering achievement – was world's largest
hydraulic bridge
two towers each 40m high
walkway 45m above river – closed in 1910 (too many
suicides)
bridge opens at least once a day – if lucky might
see it!

B | MUST TELL: **STORY / ANECDOTE**

Green Park on left
Why 'Green' Park?
No flowers – just trees and grass.
Why no flowers?
In 17th C king walked thru park –
    picked flowers for mistress
    (girlfriend)
Queen (wife) not happy – all flowers removed
Bunch of grass = not so romantic!

3 Write notes for the Top Visual Priority (a description of a famous sight) and Must Tell (an amusing story or something about the food and drink or local customs) sections for a tour in your own country or region. Remember to write only the notes, not the full text.

Speaking

Coach tour role-play

1 In pairs, prepare a tour of an area you know well. You can use or adapt the notes you made in *Writing*.
- Things to remember at start
- Top Visual Priority – description
- Must Tell – story / anecdote
- Getting off reminders

2 Work in groups of five or six. Take turns to give your commentary to the rest of the group. The 'passengers' should make notes on each guide's performance using the Standards of performance in *Vocabulary* on p.71.

Are there any items of clothing, musical instruments, or drinks which are typical of your region or country?

Listening

Problems on tour

1 🎧 Listen to a guide dealing with a problem on a coach. Which of these situations has occurred?

1 coach breaks down in the city centre

2 coach breaks down on the motorway

3 driver feels very ill and can't continue

4 one of the passengers faints

5 air-conditioning breaks down

6 one of the passengers gets very upset

2 🎧 Look at this list of guidelines given to tour guides. Listen to the guide again and tick (✓) the boxes when the guide demonstrates one of the guidelines.

Guideline

1 Listen to the customer ☐

2 Apologize ☐

3 Show sympathy and understanding ☐

4 Address the customer by name ☐

5 Explain and clarify ☐

6 Calm the person / people if they are agitated ☐

7 Solve the problem or offer a plan of action ☐

8 Use the support of colleagues and supervisors if necessary ☐

9 Make sure the customer knows exactly what you're going to do ☐

10 End the discussion ☐

3 Do you think the guide handled the situation well? Would you have done anything differently?

● Language spot

Language of calming and dealing with a crisis

1 Match these expressions from *Listening* with the guidelines in **2**.

a I'm very sorry about this, but as you can see we have a bit of a problem.

b Now, please keep calm.

c Please don't worry, Mrs Parsons.

d This is what we're going to do. We're going to …

e Oh dear, what's the matter?

f Don't worry.

g I know, I understand.

h Let me explain the situation.

i I hope that's clear?

j I'll tell you what we'll do.

2 Here are some more expressions. Match them with the guidelines.

a Oh dear, that sounds terrible. Have a seat.

b Try to relax. I'm sure it'll be all right.

c Please calm down.

d Do you all understand what we're going to do?

e Let's go and ask at the desk to see if they know anything.

f I'm afraid I'm going to have to talk to my head office.

g I don't think there's any point continuing with this discussion.

h This is the plan of action: we're going to …

3 Work in pairs. Choose one of the expressions from **1** or **2**, and say it to your partner. Your partner should respond with a different expression that does the same thing.

EXAMPLE

A *Don't worry*

B *There's nothing to worry about.*

» Go to **Grammar reference** p.123

Pronunciation

1 🎧 Listen. Which word or words are stressed most in each expression?

1 a I'm sorry about this.
  b I'm really sorry about this.
2 a There's nothing to worry about.
  b There's really nothing to worry about.
3 a That sounds terrible.
  b That sounds really terrible.
4 a I do apologize.
  b I really do apologize.

2 🎧 Now listen to these versions of the same expression. Which communicates more concern, a or b?

1 a I'm really sorry about this.
  b I'm really sorry about this.
2 a There's really nothing to worry about.
  b There's really nothing to worry about.
3 a That sounds really terrible.
  b That sounds really terrible.
4 a I really do apologize.
  b I really do apologize.

3 How are the a and b versions in **2** different? (Hint: which words are stressed most in each version?)

4 Practise saying the expressions in **1**. Pay attention to sentence stress.

Speaking

What would you say?

1 Work in pairs. Choose one of the situations from *Listening* **1**, or one from the list below (or you can invent your own). What would you say?

- You have fifty passengers on the coach, but the microphone is not working.
- Some of the passengers say they booked a tour to a historic building, but you are already heading for a theme park.
- As you are just setting off, there is loud bang from the engine and the coach stops.

2 Take turns to act out the situation with your partner. Correct each other's language and suggest ways of improving what you say and do.

Checklist

- [ ] I can explain arrangements
- [ ] I can make written notes to help with commentaries and presentations
- [ ] I can give a guided commentary
- [ ] I can deal with problems on tours

Key words

Nouns
anecdote
body language
clarity
comfort break
commentary
eye contact
first-aid kit
gesture
grats (gratuities)
guidelines
hazard
microphone
Must Tells
panoramic tour
pax
relief driver
rooming list
sense of humour
sympathy
tone
Top Visual Priority
tour manager

Next stop

1 What would you prefer to do during a beach holiday – lie around or do sports and play games?

2 What would your parents prefer to do?

3 Is there anything else you would like to do?

9 Hotel entertainment

Take off

1 Why do you think hotels need to offer entertainment facilities to their guests?

2 Which sort of entertainment do you think guests look for in

1 a city centre hotel?
2 a luxury beach resort hotel?
3 a small rural hotel?

3 Which different types of hotel entertainment have you used?

Vocabulary

Something for everyone

1 Match these hotel entertainment facilities and activities with the pictures.

1 aqua aerobics	8 pedal boat
2 cabaret	9 inline skating
3 casino	10 scuba diving
4 disco	11 spa centre
5 fitness centre	12 swimming
6 kids' club	13 video-gaming
7 pay TV	14 windsurfing

2 Classify each activity in **1**. Some activities will fit more than one category.

a sports and recreation
b indoor entertainment
c kids' entertainment
d entertainment for adults

3 Add two more activities to each category in **2**.

4 Choose the two activities you like best from each category. Tell your partner why you like them.

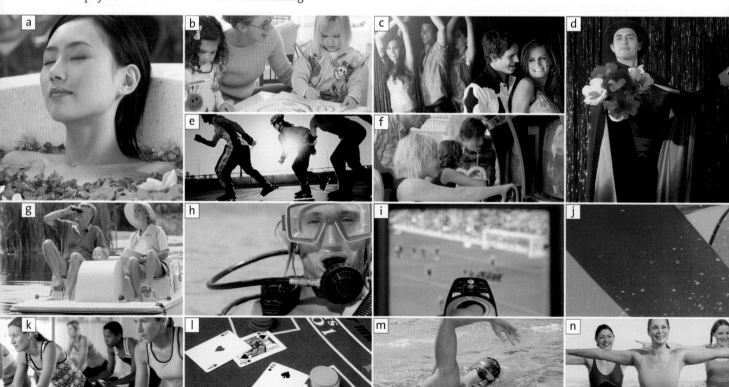

Pronunciation

1 🎧 Listen and practise saying the words below. Pay attention to the pronunciation of the consonants at the beginning of each word.

scuba diving
skating
sports
swimming

2 🎧 Now listen and practise these words. Pay attention to the pronunciation of the consonants at the end of each word.

kids
adult
practised
went

3 Now combine words from **2** with activities from **1** and say what activities there are, or what activities people did. Be careful with groups of consonants at the beginning and end of words.

EXAMPLES
The kids' scuba diving classes are in the morning.
The adult skating classes are in the sports hall.
We practised skating yesterday.
We went swimming last night.

4 Make up a tongue twister about hotel entertainment with as many consonant groups as possible.

EXAMPLE
The kids practised sports, but the adults tried scuba diving and windsurfing.

Customer care
Customers of all ages

Tourists come in all different shapes and sizes – and ages. When it comes to entertainment, different ages may have different needs. What entertainment do you think these 'seven ages of the tourist' will require? You can choose from the items in the box if you want.

1 Young children (aged 0 to 12)
2 Teenagers
3 Young adults
4 Young couples
5 Families with young kids
6 Middle-aged people
7 Retired people

> Trip to a water park or theme park
> Candlelit dinner
> Making things and playing games
> Playing tennis
> Trip to a museum or art gallery
> Waterskiing or windsurfing
> Bungee jumping or white-water rafting
> Clubbing and dancing
> Good food and drink
> Shopping

But remember: don't assume your customer will want a certain type of entertainment just because they are a particular age. There may be teenagers in your care who like to visit museums and art galleries, and there may be retired people who want to go clubbing or visit a computer-game arcade!

General rules for entertainers

- Refer to clients as 'guests'
- Try to get everyone to participate in games
- Give prizes only when somebody wins
- Don't play games with money
- Don't speak about sex, religion, or politics

Reading

What's on today

1 Look at the day's entertainment programme for the Isle of Krk hotel, in Croatia. What activities are there for

1 children early in the morning?   3 teenagers?
2 adults after lunch?

2 Which activities

1 involve competitions and games?
2 are not suitable for young children?
3 take place indoors?

3 What do you need to take for the boat trip? Why?

4 Why do you need sun cream and a T-shirt for snorkelling?

5 What looks least interesting in the programme? What would you put in its place?

● Language spot

Indefinite pronouns

1 Complete the sentences with *anyone, everyone, no one,* or *someone*.

1 Our entertainment programme has something for _____ .

2 Is there _____ who doesn't know how to swim?

3 _____ should feel that they have lost when you play games for fun.

4 In a group of adults, there will always be _____ who doesn't like games.

5 _____ who can swim can try snorkelling.

2 How do you say *anyone, everyone, no one,* and *someone* in your own language?

3 What is the difference in meaning between these words?

4 Complete these sentences.

1 A good entertainment worker is _____ who loves being with people.

2 _____ who is young, energetic, and creative can become an entertainment worker.

3 Make sure that there are questions for _____ in the family quiz.

Hotel Isle of Krk, Croatia

Tues 12 Aug

ENTERTAINMENT AND ACTIVITY PROGRAMME

Time	Age & comments	Meeting point
10.00	KidZone 10.00–13.00. Daily activity session for 3–10s	Children's pool
10.30	Learn to DJ Teens and 'older' teens	Istria Lounge
11.30	Glass-bottomed boat trips Bring sun hats, sun cream, and sunglasses	Hotel reception area
12.00	Pool madness Aqua aerobics for all. No one is too unfit for this training session gone mad	Adult pool
16.00	KidZone 16.00–19.00 p.m. Fun & games for 3–10s	Children's pool
16.00	Snorkelling in the sea Only for swimmers aged 12 and over Don't forget your T-shirt, sun cream, and towel	Terrace
17.00	Talent competition Rehearsals 10–16s only	Porec Lounge
20.00	Family quiz night Questions for everyone	Dubrovnic Suite
23.00	Dancing with KB Sounds Disco the night away	Dubrovnic Suite

4 When you are talking to a group, make sure that _____ is listening.

5 When you are talking to a group, make sure that _____ has the sun in their eyes.

6 I don't know _____ who doesn't enjoy a well-organized evening show.

» Go to **Grammar reference** p.124

Speaking

Preparing a daily programme

1 Work in pairs. Look back at *Reading*, and analyse the activities programme. Ask questions like this.

- Does the programme have something for everyone?
- Is there something to do at all times of the day?
- Are the activities varied and fun?

2 When you have identified the weak points in the programme, think of better activities.

3 Prepare a programme of events for an imaginary hotel. Think of original names for the kids' club, the activities for teenagers, and so on.

4 Work with another two pairs. Present your programme. Student A, announce the daytime activities. Student B, announce the evening activities. Say things like this:

Student A *Good morning, everyone. We hope you slept well and are ready for a lot more fun. Today's programme has something for everyone. To start the day …*

Student B *Good morning, everyone. We hope you have had a great day and are ready for a lot more fun. This evening's programme has something for everyone. To start the evening …*

Where in the world?

The MGM Grand is one of the world's biggest hotels with over 5,000 rooms. Las Vegas, of course, is famous for its casinos, but if your luck is down, is there anything else to entertain you? And what about kids? What is there for them? Read on and find out.

Guests to the MGM Grand are fascinated by the glamour and excitement of its sophisticated shows, high-class dining, and first-class nightlife. But if you want to take it easy, it's cool by the pool, once you've decided which one. This 'city of entertainment' offers its guests so much that it's more like a big-budget film studio than a place to sleep. And it's just as big. With 5,034 rooms, the $1 billion MGM Grand resort hotel offers the maximum Vegas experience.

Attractions: the Lion Habitat is a glass-enclosed area where you can watch the lions feed, play, and sleep; the CBS Television City Research Center screens new television shows daily.

Dining: try cordon-bleu cookery at The Mansion, fresh fish at Michael Mina's Seablue restaurant, the Louisiana flavor of the New Orleans Fish House, the nouvelle cuisine of the Wolfgang Puck Bar & Grill, or a taste of Italy at the Fiamma Trattoria.

Entertainment: different visiting stars at the MGM Grand Garden Arena, a 16,800-seat special events center; the Hollywood Theatre, a 740-seat theater.

Health club: stay fit or get fit. Either way, the health club has what you need.

Nightlife: choose between the Studio 54 nightclub, and the Tabúlounge. Or visit them both!

Pools: the 2,500 m² water complex features five pools, three Jacuzzis, and a unique 300m-long river pool.

Shops: Studio Walk, Star Lane Shop, Front Page News Stand, Grand Spirits, MGM Grand & Co.

Wedding chapel: Las Vegas weddings are world famous, and the Forever Grand Wedding Chapel offers once-in-a-lifetime wedding ceremony packages.

Spa: our 2,700 m² spa boasts more than 20 treatment rooms and all kinds of massages and spa services.

Child-care facilities: No.

Most of the time I was with teenagers. I know it's a difficult age but I didn't have any problems. There's a bit of a rebel in me, so when it was my turn to be with them, I really enjoyed it. There's got to be a bit of rebel in you to do this job. Conformists, no thanks!

Diego Quintero
Entertainment worker, Mallorca

Reading

Working with kids

Children's entertainment is very important in beach hotels. Children's entertainers usually need the help of their company training manual to do their job well.

1 Look at the introduction to the section on entertaining children in the manual.

  1 Why is working with kids difficult?

  2 Why is it important to keep kids entertained?

2 Match four of the points of special attention with the extracts from the manual.

3 Read the extracts again. Answer the questions.

  1 Why should an entertainer 'be a kid again'?

  2 Think of three more themes for kids' programmes.

  3 When is children's entertainment work more difficult – early in the season or in mid-season?

4 Work in groups. Think of two pieces of advice for each of the other points. Pool all your ideas with the rest of the class.

Coursebook Maximaal Entertainment   20—

KIDS' ENTERTAINMENT

Remember! Remember! Remember!

1 Working with kids is not an easy option. They have more energy than an Olympic athlete, and are more demanding than any of your bosses at Maximaal Entertainment.

2 Kids' entertainment is possibly the most important part of hotel entertainment. Why? Because happy kids make happy parents.

Always pay special attention to

- Atmosphere
- Themes
- Ability
- Safety
- Reality
- Parents.

1 We train you, but this is what you create. Make every day different and make it special. Put originality and effort into your programmes. The more you try, the more kids love you. And dress the part – dress up each day to fit the theme. Show the kids you're interested in them. Be a kid again. You'll be surprised how good it feels.

2 Each day has to be different and that can be hard for you. Don't despair. Remember that kids have great imaginations, and draw on that. Pirates, the stars, magicians, dinosaurs, monsters, and fairy tales – there are a thousand things that can make the focus for the day. And don't forget local and national festivities. They are also part of a kid's world.

3 Where there are kids, there are parents. With time, you'll see that parents aren't that hard to deal with. Welcome them and their kids in the same way – with interest and enthusiasm. Use parents where possible. And don't forget: with young kids, make sure you know where the parents are.

4 It doesn't matter how well you plan your programmes – things can change. Early or late in the season there may not be enough kids to run some activities. In the middle of the season it can get so hot that lots of kids (or their parents) want to stay indoors. This will ruin a sports or swimming day. But these are real situations and you need to accept them and adapt.

Listening

Making a water ball

1 Look at the pictures showing you how to make a water ball. Try to put them in order.

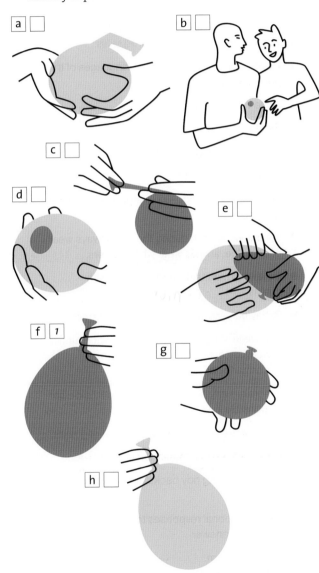

a

b

c

d

e

f 1

g

h

2 🎧 Listen to Sonia describing how to make the water ball. Check your answers.

3 🎧 Listen again and make notes.

4 Use your notes and try to tell your partner how to make a water ball.

● Language spot

Helping kids to make things

1 Look at phrases a–h from Sonia's instructions. Which phrases tell the group

1 what they have to do?

2 what they have to do and the sequence they have to follow?

a Blow up one of the balloons to stretch it a little.

b Now, once you've stretched the balloon, fill it with water and tie a knot.

c When you tie the knot, make the shape of the balloon as round as possible.

d Do you see what I mean?

e Now get another balloon, blow it up, let the air out …

f … when you've let the air out, place the first balloon inside it.

g Work in twos and help each other.

h Have you all done that?

2 We use the imperative to tell people what to do. What other verb tenses has Sonia used?

3 Look at c and f. They both begin with *when* and they both describe two actions. Which phrase describes

1 Action 1 and *next* Action 2?

2 Action 1 and *at the same time* Action 2?

≫ Go to **Grammar reference** p.125

Speaking

Getting kids to make things

1 Work in pairs. Student A, go to p.109. Student B, go to p.111. Study the instructions. Make sure you understand them completely. Think carefully about the language you are going to use to explain the activity.

2 Take turns to be the entertainment worker. Your partner will listen and carry out the instructions.

3 When you finish, discuss how well you did with your partner. Did you have any problems giving instructions? Were the instructions and the sequence clear to your partner? Did you offer help and encouragement?

Listening

Getting the job

🎧 Listen to Ineke talking about how she got a job as a hotel entertainer in Bali, Indonesia. Answer the questions.

1 Why did she want to work as a hotel entertainer?
2 How did she find the job in Bali?
3 What happened at the initial selection?
4 Which of the following techniques does Ineke say she practised during the training session?

   a using the right tone of voice
   b using a microphone
   c keeping groups under control
   d how to stand on stage
   e how to organize games
   f elementary first aid

5 Which did Ineke enjoy more – the training or the job? How do you know?

Vocabulary

The perfect worker

1 Hotel entertainment work requires a special personality, specific skills, and accepting company rules. Look at the points describing the perfect entertainment worker. Which points are about
   1 qualities and skills?   3 worker–guest relations?
   2 company rules?

2 Measure your own personality against that of the perfect entertainment worker. Where are you strong, and where are you weak?

Coursebook Maximaal Entertainment 20–

The perfect entertainment worker

1 Have good public relations (PR) skills.

2 Have a good command of the languages of the hotel's guests.

3 Have initiative. Be creative.

4 Be able to work in a team.

5 Have a charismatic personality.

6 Have an open nature.

7 Physical appearance – no sunglasses, no large piercings.

8 Wear your uniform during the day. Always wear your badge; always wear white trainers.

9 Be able to maintain a conversation with guests.

10 Behaviour – always greet guests and smile.

11 Behaviour – don't smoke, drink, or eat during a performance, not even water, until the performance has finished.

12 If there are any problems, always tell the person responsible in your team.

13 Never argue with a colleague in front of guests.

14 Keep relations with other hotel workers good.

15 Keep everything tidy backstage and in the mini-club.

16 Avoid emotional responses to guests. Think before you answer.

17 Trust your team.

18 Be careful about how you say things and about gestures and posture.

19 Be patient.

20 Don't discriminate between guests.

Find out

1 What activities could you use with guests of different ages in an entertainment programme? For kids, try talking to teachers at a primary school. For teenagers, think about yourselves a few years ago. For adults, talk to your parents or your teachers.

2 Work in groups. Produce an instruction sheet for each activity, and then put all of the ideas together to create your own entertainment training manual. You might want to add an appendix with the language from this unit in English and your mother tongue.

Writing

Email application

Most hotel entertainment jobs today ask you to apply online, sending a photo and CV.

```
┌──────────────────────────────────────── _ □ × ┐
│                                                  │
│  Hotel Entertainers / Children's Entertainers    │
│  Location: Greek Isles   Job Category: Hotel     │
│  entertainment                                   │
│  Job Details: We are looking for dynamic young   │
│  people to work as part of a team providing      │
│  entertainment in our resort hotels in the Greek │
│  Islands. You will be helping to programme and   │
│  run the hotel entertainment programme.          │
│  Daytime duties include the kids' games and      │
│  sports activities, CrazyKidsClub for young      │
│  children, keep fit, and aerobics sessions.      │
│  Evening duties include mini-disco for kids, fun │
│  dancing, karaoke, and quizzes for families, and │
│  games sessions, dances, and shows for adults.   │
│  Experience required: MUST have good knowledge   │
│  of at least one European language (English,     │
│  French, German, Italian, Dutch) and be able to  │
│  speak at least one other European language.     │
│  Full training, transport, and living costs      │
│  provided.                                       │
│  To apply online, [ click here. ]                │
└──────────────────────────────────────────────────┘
```

1 Think about your own personality and skills. Organize your ideas into separate groups. When you write, these groups will be separate paragraphs.

2 Prepare an email applying for the job. If you want, go to p.56 and look at the email there to help you.

Checklist

Assess your progress in this unit. Tick (✓) the statements which are true.

- [ ] I can prepare an entertainment programme for a beach resort hotel

- [ ] I can describe how to make simple arts and crafts objects to a group of children

- [ ] I can understand texts about training for entertainment work

- [ ] I can write an email applying for a job as an entertainment worker

Key words

Activities programme
aqua aerobics
cabaret
casino
disco
fitness centre
pay TV
pedal boat
quiz
scuba diving
snorkelling
video-gaming

People
adult
couple
kid
retired person
teenager

Perfect worker
badge
charismatic
initiative
posture
public relations (PR)
uniform

Next stop

1 Do you have any hobbies or special interests? How could a tour operator provide a tour that involved your hobby or interest?

2 What types of holidays do elderly people like to go on? Think about members of your own family.

10 Specialized tourism

Take off

1 How are these photos connected to tourism?

2 Can you think of any holidays that would include these experiences?

scenior

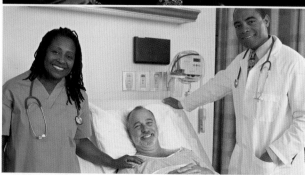

medical tourism

Reading

What is niche tourism?

1 Read the text. Which is growing faster: mass tourism or niche tourism?

2 Do you know what all the 'micro-niches' are? Which ones

   1 are geared towards students and young people?
      Educational Sport
   2 help tourists to find out about their ancestors?
      Heritage Tribal Reserch Geneology
   3 get tourists working on environmentally-friendly projects?

   4 involve being either a participant or a spectator?

   5 involve eating and drinking?

3 Here are some more niches. What do you think each of them involves? Where would you put them on the chart?

   1 industrial
   2 plane-spotting
   3 cosmetic surgery
   4 film trail

Inside tourism: mass tourism – niche tourism

Mass tourism has grown at a remarkable pace in the last fifty years – more leisure time, more tourists, more resorts, bigger hotel complexes, more attractions able to take huge numbers of visitors, larger aircraft, many more flights. But in contrast to this, as people have travelled more, the need to experience something different, something special, something tailored to the specific needs and interests of individuals and groups of individuals, has also grown. The result is 'niche tourism': tour operators have realized there is a market for the

specialist tourist, and it is a market that often spends more than the 'package-holiday' tourist. This market is perhaps the fastest-growing market in the tourism industry.

Niche tourism has a thousand different faces – holidays for senior citizens, tours for the disabled, gastronomic holidays, tours geared towards the gay community, photographic holidays, 'dark' tourism (visiting places with sinister and macabre histories), and many more. The chart below lists some of the niches.

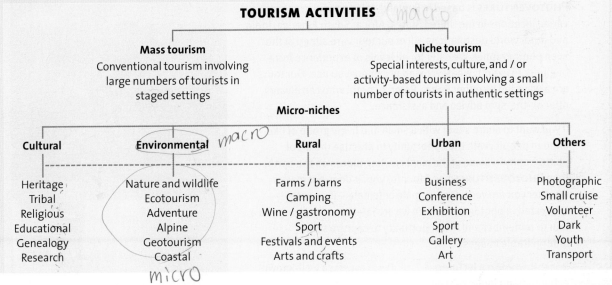

TOURISM ACTIVITIES (macro

Mass tourism	**Niche tourism**
Conventional tourism involving large numbers of tourists in staged settings	Special interests, culture, and / or activity-based tourism involving a small number of tourists in authentic settings

Micro-niches

Cultural	**Environmental** macro	**Rural**	**Urban**	**Others**
Heritage	Nature and wildlife	Farms / barns	Business	Photographic
Tribal	Ecotourism	Camping	Conference	Small cruise
Religious	Adventure	Wine / gastronomy	Exhibition	Volunteer
Educational	Alpine	Sport	Sport	Dark
Genealogy	Geotourism	Festivals and events	Gallery	Youth
Research	Coastal	Arts and crafts	Art	Transport

micro

4 Match the niches in **3** with these extracts from tour operator websites.

a Follow in the footsteps of the boy wizard, visit Alnwick Castle, the location for Hogwarts, and see where Harry Potter learnt to fly his magic broomstick.

b We will aim to see the latest range of aircraft used by the Greek Air Force.

c From an insider's glimpse of a hi-tech car plant to the weird antiquity of a Cuban cigar factory, going behind the scenes to learn how everyday consumer products are created is very enlightening.

d Recovery time is important, but it is also an opportunity to relax and enjoy some of the beautiful tourist features of the region.

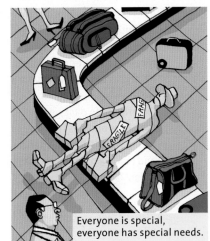
Everyone is special, everyone has special needs.

In a globalising world of increasing sameness, niche tourism represents diversity and ways of marking differences.
Marina Novelli
Senior Lecturer,
Centre for Tourism Policy Studies

It's my job

1 What type of tours do 'Photoventures' organize?

2 What are the advantages of having experts in the subject organizing and guiding tours?

3 Are there any disadvantages?

4 What other tourism services will groups going on Photoventures tours require?

5 Visit the website www.photoventures.net. Choose a tour. What encounters (between the tour party and tourism professionals) will be involved?

6 Which photo do you like best?

PHOTOVENTURES is owned and operated by Roger Reynolds Hon. FRPS and Peter Morss ARPS and organizes specialist tours with the photographer in mind.

PHOTOVENTURES is based in England, taking small groups to varied locations in the United States, Africa, South America, India, and other world destinations. All of our tours are aimed at the keen photographer. We cater for all levels of experience from beginner to expert, whatever kind of camera you use. Our tours are always led by either Roger, Peter, or both, who can always offer on-the-spot advice and assistance.

If you want to share a tour with a small and lively group of like-minded people, with the opportunity to practise the art of photography in some of the most exciting places on the earth, then **PHOTOVENTURES** has a tour for you. It does not matter whether you are young or old, male or female – if you are interested in photography, then we are interested in giving you a tour to remember and the opportunity to capture some unforgettable images.

Roger Reynolds: a lecturer, exhibitor, and judge with an international reputation. He has exhibited internationally for over twenty years and has received hundreds of awards. He prides himself on having a wealth of expertise and experience to pass on to tour members and has travelled extensively in North America and made a number of visits to India.

Peter Morss: a well-known photographic lecturer and judge. His work has been accepted in numerous International and National Exhibitions. He has travelled extensively in the United States and has a wide knowledge of many parts of this vast, beautiful country.

Listening

Special requests

🎧 Listen to five dialogues between a tourist and a guide.

1 Match each dialogue with one of the tour logos.

2 In each dialogue, what request is the tourist making?

3 Will the guide be able to meet the request?

a

b

Gastro-adventures

Religious buildings of Central Europe

c

Photo-tours

d

Flora and fauna of South America

e

Industrial Africa

● Language spot

Responding to special requests

1 🎧 Listen to the dialogues again and complete these phrases.

1 That _____ be a problem.

2 Sorry, you _____ .

3 You _____ remove them.

4 Of course. No _____ .

5 I don't see _____ . There _____ be a problem if …

6 You _____ need to pay something.

7 I'm not _____ .

8 We _____ be able to make arrangements.

2 In which of the phrases is the guide saying

a definitely yes?   c possibly yes?

b probably yes?   d definitely no?

3 Which of the modal verbs a–e mean the following?

1 It's a possibility.   a can't

2 It's against the rules.   b may

3 It's impossible.   c might

4 It's unlikely.   d mustn't

                              e shouldn't

≫ Go to **Grammar reference** p.125

Speaking

Four specialized tours

1 Work in pairs. What do you think these specialized tours involve? Where could they take place? What special services might tourists require?

1 Adventure sports – diving

2 Life-seeing tourism

3 Medical tourism

4 Genealogy tourism

2 Find out about the tours. Student A, go to p.109. Student B, go to p.114. Tell each other about the tours.

3 Match these requests for special services with the four tours in **1**.

a Visit a criminal court and meet a group of lawyers.

b Get special access to records kept in the local Town Hall.

c Go out on a trip to deeper waters.

d Health spa with meditation classes.

e Visit a traditional working farm to see how people worked a hundred years ago.

f Consultation with a doctor for possible weight-reduction surgery.

g Have a guided tour of a hospital.

h Find out more about opportunities for working as a qualified instructor.

4 Choose one of the special services and role-play conversations between a tourist and a tour guide, as in the *Listening* and *Language spot*.

The best way of finding out the needs of customers with disabilities is the same as for all customers: ask them!
Ray Jackson
Art gallery guide – and wheelchair-user

Vocabulary

Describing disability

1 Read these statements. Write T (true) or F (false).

1 Most disabled people need a wheelchair.

2 If you see someone with a hearing-aid, you should raise your voice.

3 People with hearing difficulties can hear some people better than others.

4 Someone who is reading a newspaper cannot be visually-impaired.

5 Most blind people have guide dogs and know how to read Braille.

6 People who use sign language cannot speak.

7 In many countries it is illegal to discriminate against people with disabilities.

8 In my country all public places must provide full access to disabled people, for example, ramps on steps for wheelchairs, and hand-rails for people with mobility difficulties.

2 Here are some disabilities that tourists may have. Match the disability with the tourist statements below. There may be more than one possibility.

1 mobility difficulty
2 wheelchair user
3 hearing impairment
4 visual impairment

a 'I need a room on the ground floor.'
b 'Could you help me across the road?'
c 'Can you speak a bit louder, please? I'm a bit deaf.'
d 'Can you pass it down to me to sign? I can't reach the desk from here.'
e 'I'm afraid I can't read the print on this form.'
f 'I just need you to go a little slower.'
g 'You'll have to use sign language.'
h 'He can't see anything at all.'

3 What problems could disabled tourists have with these facilities?

1 single steps
2 stairs
3 telephone
4 toilets
5 hotel check-in (and check-out)
6 restaurants
7 car parks
8 gates
9 visiting a castle or ancient monument
10 footpaths in the countryside
11 beaches
12 welcome talks

4 How (and who) could the following items help?

1 lift
2 hand-rail
3 ramp
4 signs in large print
5 signs in Braille
6 low-level light switches
7 low-level reception desk
8 wide doorways
9 specially-adapted walkways
10 motorized buggy
11 remote control opening device

Pronunciation

1 Look at these words. Which syllable is stressed?

1 car park
2 guide dog
3 doorway
4 footpath
5 hand-rail
6 health spa
7 hearing aid
8 light switch
9 sign language
10 walkway
11 welcome talk
12 wheelchair

2 🎧 Listen and check your answers, then practise the pronunciation.

3 🎧 Now do the same with these words.

1 specially adapted
2 purpose-built
3 hearing impaired
4 remote control

4 Choose the correct word in *italics* to complete the rules.

1 Compounds created from two nouns often have the stress on the *first / second* noun.

2 Other types of compound usually have the stress on the *first / second* word.

A person is not disabled by their impairment, but by the environment and the attitudes of the people they encounter.
Tourism for All Campaign

Listening

Disability access

A group of tourists with mobility disabilities are on a special tour involving adventure sports. They are staying at an old country hotel, which has recently been renovated to allow access for all.

1 🎧 The tour guide is phoning ahead to check arrangements. Listen to the conversation and tick (✓) the disabled facilities that are currently in operation at the hotel.

   1 Access for wheelchairs to ground floor rooms ☐
   2 Automatic door opening on ground floor rooms ☐
   3 Low-level light switches in ground floor rooms ☐
   4 Disabled facilities in toilets ☐
   5 Signage ☐
   6 Lift to top floor bar ☐
   7 Garden walkways and general access ☐
   8 Low-level reception desk ☐
   9 Entrance access (ramps, etc.) ☐

2 After they leave the hotel, the group are going by coach to an adventure sports activity centre, where they are planning to do some of the following activities – hillwalking, rowing, canoeing, overnight camping. What facilities will the guide need to check with the coach company and the activity centre?

● Language spot

Identifying and checking special needs

1 Look at picture 1. What needs to be done to the hotel to make it accessible to people with disabilities?

   EXAMPLE
   reception area (renovate) The reception area needs renovating / to be renovated.

   doors (widen)

   ramps (install)

   lift (repair)

   etc.

   ≫ Go to **Grammar reference** p.126

2 Look at picture 2. What has been done?

   EXAMPLE   *The reception area has been renovated.*

   ≫ Go to **Grammar reference** p.126

3 A tour guide is bringing a group of tourists with disabilities to the hotel. She last visited when it was like picture 1. Write the questions she will ask, and then act out the conversation she has with the hotel to check the facilities for her group.

   EXAMPLES
   Has the hotel been renovated?
   Are there guest rooms on the ground floor?

4 Use the information you noted in *Listening* **2** to role-play the conversations between the tour guide and (a) the coach company, and (b) the manager of the adventure sports activity centre.

How many specialist holidays can you think of where binoculars would be an important piece of equipment?

Find out

1 How does your region or country cater for specialized tourism?

2 Are there any tour operators who organize tours and holidays for any of the niches listed in *Reading* on p.85?

3 Make a data-file for each of the niches. Include
  - contact details of tour operators
  - description of tours
  - special facilities that are used (e.g. accommodation, transport)
  - what is included / not included in the tour price
  - whether they cater for disability
  - what makes the tour 'special'.

4 Do you think there are any other niches that could be catered for? Is there a 'gap in the market'? Think about your own hobbies and interests.

Writing

Report on specialized tourism

Write up the results of your research in *Find out* using the following template.

Speaking

Preparing and running a specialized tour

Work in groups. Plan a niche tour in your own country or region. Work through each of the following stages.

Stage 1: Choose a niche
  - Try to choose something different and exciting, but relevant to your area.
  - The tour should be available to disabled as well as able-bodied people.

Stage 2: Plan the tour
  - What makes it special?
  - Decide the specialized and general tourism activities you are going to offer.
  - Decide the transport and accommodation arrangements you are going to offer.
  - Map out the basic itinerary.

Stage 3: Brief the staff involved
  - What staff are going to be involved in the tour?
  - What special training will they need?

Stage 4: Presentation
  - Present your tour in detail to another group.

Specialized tourism in _____

Type of specialized tourism

Tour operator

Contact details

What's included

Disabled facilities

Why it's special

Recommendation / star rating

Case study of a tour

Title of tour

Tour operator

Description of tour

Accommodation

Transport arrangements

Proposal for a new specialized tour

Title of tour

Description

What's included

Why it's special

Checklist

Assess your progress in this unit. Tick (✓) the statements which are true.

- I can talk about the range of specialized tours involved in niche tourism
- I can respond to and act on special requests
- I can understand the issues involved in dealing with disability and tourism
- I can identify and check special needs
- I can write a report on specialized tourism

Key words

Descriptions of disability
blind
deaf
hearing impairment
learning difficulty
visual impairment

Other nouns
cosmetic surgery
genealogy
mobility
niche
signage

Facilities for the disabled
access
Braille
guide dog
hand-rail
hearing aid
low-level
ramp
sign language
walkway
wheelchair

Verbs
discriminate
renovate

Next stop

1 Have you, or has anyone you know, ever travelled away from home as part of your work or study?

2 How was the experience different from a holiday? Did you feel different? Did you need any different services or facilities?

3 If your place of study was planning a study trip to another country, where would you like to go?

Customer care
Cross-cultural misunderstandings

Some niches are very specialized and unusual, and sometimes they will not be understood by the host community. Cultural differences and misunderstandings like this can often occur when working in tourism.

Read about one group of niche tourists whose hobby was not understood, and who found themselves in serious trouble.

1 What was the niche interest of the tourists?
2 What went wrong?
3 What could the tourism professionals (tour operator, tour guide, etc.) have done to avoid the problems?
4 What misunderstandings – cultural or otherwise – do you think could occur on some of the other specialist holidays we have looked at in this unit?

Plane-spotters cleared of spying

Eleven British and two Dutch plane-spotters, who were given prison sentences for spying in Greece, have been allowed to go free.

The group were arrested one year ago as they took notes at an air base open day in Kalamata, Greece.

Paul Coppin, the tour operator who arranged the trip, was one of the arrested group. He said that it had been a misunderstanding and that it was obvious that they were not spies, but that they were just doing their hobby.

Squadron Leader Nektarios Samara, of the Greek Air Force, said their actions could be dangerous for the security of the country. He had no idea that plane-spotting was a hobby and that it was allowed in other countries.

11 Business travel

Take off

1 Look at the figures on inbound and outbound business travel to and from the UK.

INBOUND	%
Business travel as % of all travel to UK	26.7%
Region of origin:	
North America	13.1%
EU Europe	67.4%
Non-EU Europe	5.9%
Rest of world	13.6%

OUTBOUND	%
Business travel as % of all travel from UK	15.8%
Region visited:	
North America	9.6%
EU Europe	73.2%
Non-EU Europe	9.0%
Rest of world	8.2%

2 Do you think the figures would be different for your country? How could you find out?

3 What do business travellers do when they come to your country, for example, *meetings, conferences*?

4 Which type of businesses do they visit? Think of the names of two or three large companies in your country that might be involved in international business travel.

In this unit
- business travel terms
- cultural awareness
- conferences and exhibitions
- jobs in business travel

Vocabulary

Business travel terms

1 The acronym MICE is often used to describe the different parts of the business travel industry. What do you think the letters stand for?

2 Look at the table and find the four words, beginning with M, I, C, and E which mean the following.

1 occasions when people come together to discuss or decide something – usually involving a small number of people

2 journeys or holidays given to a worker or group of workers as rewards for good work

3 large official meetings, usually lasting for a few days, at which people with the same work or interests come together to discuss their views

4 events at which products and services produced by different companies are shown to the public

Individual business travel	Business tourism
● Presentations	● Meetings and seminars
	● Conferences
	● Product launches
● Consultations	● Incentive trips (team, family)
● Investigations	● Exhibitions (trade fairs, trade shows, consumer shows)
● One-to-one meetings	● Corporate hospitality (spectator, participative)

3 Match the following events (a–e) with items from the table. Then complete the sentences (1–5) with the words or phrases below.

delegates	a PowerPoint presentation	box
stands	gala banquet	

a _____ : The World Federation of Tour Guides is meeting in Hong Kong to discuss a number of issues affecting their business and to hear talks from key representatives of the industry. There will be _____ [1] from all over the world.

b _____ : Hammond Brothers Ltd are pleased to announce their new 'Green machine' power-cycle, ideal for the business person and the weary sightseeing tourist alike. Come to the Meeting Room of the Imperial Hotel for _____ [2] by the Chief Designer and the Sales Manager. Drinks and snacks will be provided.

c _____ : Join us for the final of the Rugby League World Cup for champagne and a superb buffet lunch. Watch the game from the comfort and luxury of our own private _____ [3].

d _____ : As a reward for achieving record sales figures in the last financial year, the Directors of General Instruments Inc. are delighted to invite you on a tour of the capitals of Western Europe. On the final evening the CEO will attend the _____ [4] to personally thank you.

e _____ : FITUR is the world's largest travel show after ITB Berlin. There are three trade days (with 75,000 professional visitors expected) and two consumer days (with 150,000 visitors expected). FITUR is also the major event for Latin American tour operators contracting their European tours. Industry partners can hire _____ [5] for five days for approx €4,000.

Find out

Find out about business travel to and from your country.

1 Contact your National Tourist Office or search on the Internet to find out similar statistics to those for the UK in *Take off*.

2 Research some of the large companies in your country to see if they are involved in any of the business travel events identified in the table in *Vocabulary*.

3 What job opportunities are there in your country related to business travel? For example: at trade fairs or exhibitions, at corporate hospitality events, in 'meet and greet'.

An exhibitor at a trade fair was giving green hats to those who visited the stand. One Chinese visitor refused to accept one and looked angry. The exhibitors later learned that although green is a positive colour in China, the expression 'He wears a green hat' is used to imply a man is unfaithful to his wife or girlfriend.

Customer care

Cultural awareness

Read the cultural advice given by a tour operator to clients on one of their tours to Egypt.

> One of the most outstanding features of the Egyptian people is that of generous hospitality. To an Arab, hospitality is more than good manners; it is a matter of honour and they regard it as a sacred duty.
>
> Remember that Egypt is an Islamic country. Observe their customs and dress code in order not to cause offence. Modest clothing, which covers arms, shoulders, and legs, is recommended.

1 Did you know about these aspects of Egyptian / Arabic culture? Does any of the information surprise you?

2 What advice would you give to tourists coming to your country about hospitality, behaviour, and dress code?

Listening

The needs of the business traveller

1 Which of these are more important for business travellers than for non-business tourists and travellers?

1 time to choose from different travel options
2 possibility to make reservations at short notice
3 access to reservations 24 hours a day
4 express check-in at airports
5 packaged travel arrangements – flight, transfer, accommodation, meals, etc. all included
6 fast internet connections in hotels
7 hotel in a quiet relaxing location
8 support information on local area and culture

2 ⌒ Carlos Lozano is a travel agent specializing in business travel. Listen to the interview. Which of the items in **1** does he say are more important for the business traveller?

3 ⌒ Listen again.

1 What is the role of the account manager?
2 How does Carlos's company 'go the extra mile'?

4 What topics would you expect to be included in a 'Culture guide' covering basics of social etiquette and doing business with different cultures?

Reading

Culture guide

1 Look at the text. Match these tips with some of the categories in the Cultural etiquette section.

a Leaving food on your plate is considered rude.
b When someone meets you for the first time, they may give you their business card. Always look at it carefully and keep it on the desk in front of you.
c When shopping, it is inappropriate to bargain. Shop assistants will give you your change on a tray without counting it in front of you.
d Do not eat or drink while walking on the street.
e Tipping in restaurants is not usual. In fact if a tip is offered, it may be refused.
f If you are given a present, do not open it in front of the person who gave it to you.

2 All of these tips are from the guide to one country. Can you guess which country it is?

3 Answer the questions.

1 Do you agree that such notes will be especially useful for business travellers?
2 Are all the categories relevant to all tourists? Which ones are not?
3 Do you think it's better to use an interpreter or to speak a common language?
4 Do you think your spoken English is too formal or not formal enough?

4 Write some 'cultural etiquette' tips for your country or region (or a country that you know well). Try to write one tip for each of the categories in the text.

A guide to culture and language for the business traveller

These notes and guidelines are for anyone travelling to a country which they are not familiar with. However, as a business traveller you may find them especially useful, partly because you'll probably have more encounters with local people when doing business, and also because more may depend on them – a contract could be won by getting the cultural etiquette right.

Cultural etiquette

1 Greetings and introductions
2 Small talk / topics of conversation
3 Dress
4 Behaviour in public
5 Appointments and punctuality
6 Behaviour in meetings
7 Shopping
8 Dining out
9 Paying for meals / tipping
10 Gift-giving

Advice on language

1 Always try to learn a few words of the language of the country you are visiting, even if it's just *Hello*, *Thank you*, and *Goodbye*.

2 Find out beforehand what language you will be speaking with your hosts. If it's English, find out if their level is the same as yours. Check whether you need interpreting services.

3 If you're speaking English, remember not just to get the vocabulary and grammar as correct as possible, but also to get the level of formality right – be appropriate and polite, not too casual or informal.

Where in the world?

1 Which of the types of business travel listed in the table on p.93 do you think the Metropolitan could cater for?

2 Choose one of the companies from *Find out*. Imagine they are planning to hold a conference in Asia. Select five features or facilities at the Metropolitan that would be attractive to the company.

Metropolitan Hotel Nikko
New Delhi

The Metropolitan Hotel Nikko New Delhi offers guests a unique blend of Indian and Asian hospitality. Designed for the international business and upscale leisure traveller, the hotel is distinguished by understated elegance. A five-star deluxe international-class luxury hotel, it is strategically located in the heart of the business and commercial hub of New Delhi.

Facilities
- High-speed wi-fi Internet
- State-of-the-art business centre
- Award-winning restaurants and bar
- A health and spa centre
- Swimming pool
- Barber / beauty salon
- Laundry / valet services
- A 24-hour travel desk

Conference halls
- Spacious conference halls with high ceilings
- Conference halls with ample natural light
- Well equipped with various audio-visual facilities
- Videoconferencing facility
- Conference halls supported by break-out rooms
- Dedicated and personalized staff
- Pre-function area
- Business centre facility on the same floor

Business services
- Private meeting rooms
- Provision for laptops
- Mobile phone connection
- High-speed wi-fi internet cards
- STD/ISD facility
- Collect calls
- Teleconference calls
- Cyber café
- Secretarial services
- Japanese language translation
- Fax, photocopy, scanning, lamination, spiral binding, and other facilities available on request

Vocabulary

Conference equipment and facilities

1 Match the words or phrases 1–9 with the definitions a–i.

1 audio-visual	6 laptop
2 break-out room	7 teleconferencing
3 digital projector	8 videoconferencing
4 flip chart	9 wi-fi
5 lamination	

a technology without wires that allows several computers to share the same fast internet connection

b small computer that can work without wires and be easily carried

c system that makes paper documents into plastic documents

d equipment to show visual information (using modern computer technology)

e technology using both sound and pictures

f meeting or discussion between two or more people in different places using telephones, television, or computers

g a system that enables people in different places to have a meeting by watching and listening to each other by using computers and video cameras

h a place for a meeting of a smaller group of people away from the main meeting

i large sheets of paper fixed at the top used for presenting information at a talk or meeting

2 Look at the conference room seating plans (or configurations). Match the titles, descriptions, and plans.

Titles

Boardroom	Classroom	Theatre
Circle of chairs	Clusters	U-shape

Descriptions

a Good for large numbers needing to work on small group discussions and projects. Allows maximum participation within groups.

b One-way communication. Good for audio-visual and lecture-style presentations where note-taking is not so important.

c Gives sense of equal status at same time as allowing up-front presentation. Good for close interaction and working in pairs.

d Good for small groups where close interaction and a lot of discussion is expected. The shared table creates a sense of unity.

e Effective set up for one-way communication and large groups. It provides a work surface for note-taking and reference materials.

f Good for full involvement and face-to-face communication where there is no need for a dominant leader. Ideal for up to twenty participants. Tables can be added.

Plans

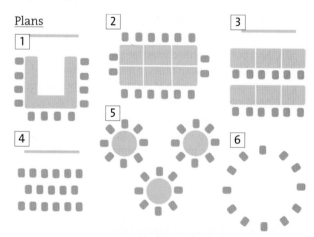

3 Which arrangement would be suitable for the following events?

1 lecture or speech	5 board meeting
2 presentation (e.g. PowerPoint)	6 wedding banquet
3 product launch	7 press conference
4 workshop or seminar	8 signing ceremony

The conventions and meeting business in the USA is a huge **$82 billion-a-year** industry. The average convention delegate stays 4.1 days and spends over **$895 per event**.

Total expenditure includes money spent on hotel rooms, restaurants, retail stores, taxis, car rentals, and other expenses.

Pronunciation

1 Match the words with the pictures.

1 pear	3 peach	5 Ben
2 bear	4 beach	6 pen

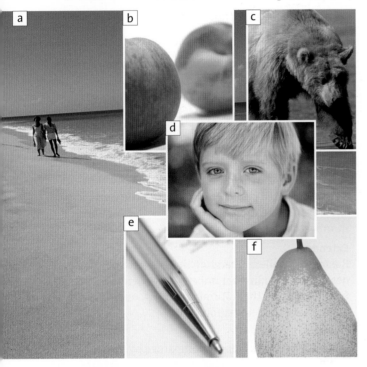

2 🎧 Listen. Which do you hear – a or b?

	1	2	3	4	5	6
a	*pear*	*pear*	*peach*	*peach*	*pen*	*pen*
b	*bear*	*bear*	*beach*	*beach*	*Ben*	*Ben*

3 🎧 Check the answers and listen again. What is the difference between the sound /p/ and the sound /b/?

4 Practise these words.

people	technology	conference
power	telephone	clusters
point	television	camera
product	talk	connection
presentation	tour	classroom

5 Make up sentences using as many words as possible from **4**. Say your sentences, paying attention to the pronunciation of /p/, /t/, and /k/.

● Language spot

Describing dimensions, capacity, and facilities

1 Complete these sentences with phrases from the box below. There is often more than one match.

1 The room is equipped with …
2 The room measures …
3 The room can seat …
4 There are …
5 The dimensions of the room are …
6 The room can seat up to …
7 The room contains …
8 We have got …
9 The room has a capacity of …
10 We can provide …

---

a a projector, a computer, and an internet connection
b 20 metres by 30 metres
c up to 300 people
d refreshments
e break-out rooms on all floors
f 10 metres wide and 35 metres long
g toilets and restrooms outside every main conference room
h 40 delegates comfortably
i an interactive whiteboard as well as a flip chart

---

2 Can you think of another way of ending each sentence?

3 Which sentences are describing
a dimensions?
b capacity?
c facilities and equipment?

4 Draw a suite of conference rooms, including seating arrangement, dimensions, capacity, and equipment. Don't show it to your partner. Your partner will ask questions and draw your suite.

EXAMPLE
What are the dimensions of the main conference room?

≫ Go to **Grammar reference** p.126

Speaking

Comparing conference centres

Work in groups of three. Find out about three hotels with conference and corporate facilities. Student A, go to p.113. Student B, go to p.114. Student C, go to p.117.

1 Describe the conference facilities to each other and make notes on the following areas.

- Name and location
- Hotel facilities
- Conference rooms and facilities
- Other conference services
- Corporate hospitality
- Other business services
- Extra events and activities

2 In groups, decide which of the conference venues, if any, would be suited to the companies you looked at in *Find out*.

3 Which of the venues would you like to work at? What job do you think you could do?

Reading

Business travel and the tourism industry

1 In pairs, discuss how business travel can benefit the tourism industry in a particular destination.

EXAMPLE *increased hotel occupancy*

2 Read the text to see if any of your ideas are mentioned.

Inside tourism: combining business with pleasure

The first major way in which business travel benefits tourism in general is that it brings more business to travel agents, transport providers, and hotels. Travel for business-related purposes can increase the level of leisure and recreational activity at the destination in a number of ways.

Extenders

Business travellers extending their visit to the destination – adding a number of days before or after – in order to enjoy the cultural, shopping, or sightseeing resources of the destination.

Guests

Business travellers being accompanied by guests (usually spouses or families) who engage in leisure tourism activities such as sightseeing excursions while at the destination.

Social programme

Business travellers themselves engaging in leisure or recreational activities as part of the social, networking, or relaxation element of the event attended.

Returners

Business travellers who have been impressed by the destination returning with their spouses or families for holidays or short breaks, or encouraging others to do so.

The second major way in which business travel benefits tourism is that it provides employment. Often this work is temporary – helping at conferences, trade fairs, or hospitality events – but these jobs can lead to longer term work and careers in tourism.

Checklist

Assess your progress in this unit. Tick (✓) the statements which are true.

- I can understand and talk about the structure of the business travel sector
- I can understand the importance of being aware of cultural differences
- I can describe conference facilities

3 Are these activities and tours examples of 'extenders', 'guests', 'social programme', or 'returners'?

1 Edinburgh: Special whisky-tasting evening for delegates

2 Vancouver: Come and see us again! Bring the family and get a discount

3 Istanbul: While you work – sightseeing excursion for your partner

4 Helsinki: Post-conference three-day Lapland tour

4 What extender, guest, and social programme activities would you include for a conference in your city or region?

Writing

A conference enquiry

Choose one of the four hotels we have looked at in the *Where in the world?* and *Speaking* sections.

Write an email reply to the representative of a company enquiring about conference facilities. You are going to attach full details of your conference facilities, but you should answer the enquirer's direct questions in your email.

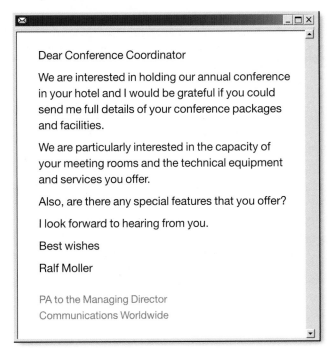

Dear Conference Coordinator

We are interested in holding our annual conference in your hotel and I would be grateful if you could send me full details of your conference packages and facilities.

We are particularly interested in the capacity of your meeting rooms and the technical equipment and services you offer.

Also, are there any special features that you offer?

I look forward to hearing from you.

Best wishes

Ralf Moller

PA to the Managing Director
Communications Worldwide

Key words

Nouns
boardroom
break-out room
capacity
configuration
corporate hospitality
delegate
dimension
exhibition
flip chart
gala banquet
lamination
laptop
presentation
product launch
projector / digital projector
stand
teleconferencing
videoconferencing

Adjectives
audio-visual
theatre-style
U-shaped
wi-fi

Next stop

1 What are the worst experiences you have had as a customer?

2 Did you complain? If you did, what happened? If you didn't complain, explain why not.

3 Have you ever needed to make a complaint about poor service in a hotel? What happened?

12 Checking out

Take off

In tourism today, it is vital to know how your customer feels about your services. Look at the hotel customer satisfaction form.

1 Which aspects of hotel service can you see?

2 Which other areas of the hotel's services and facilities do you think will be on the form?

3 The form has a space at the bottom for the guest to make suggestions. What do you think are the most common suggestions?

4 What are the commonest causes of complaints in hotels?

FAIRMONT HOTEL DURBAN

We sincerely hope that you have enjoyed your stay in the Fairmont, where our principal aim is to offer you better and better service every day. To help us do this, we would be very grateful if you could spare us a few minutes and let us know how well we have done.

REASON FOR VISIT

Business ☐   Conference ☐   Tourism ☐

How many nights a month do you use the Fairmont?   1 to 5 ☐   5 to 10 ☐   More than 10 ☐

	Very satisfied	Quite satisfied	Acceptable	Not satisfied	Poor
1 Overall rating of hotel	☐	☐	☐	☐	☐
2 Room	☐	☐	☐	☐	☐
3 Decoration	☐	☐	☐	☐	☐
4 Bed & pillows	☐	☐	☐	☐	☐
5 Cleanliness	☐	☐	☐	☐	☐

Please note here any suggestions you would like to make as to how we can improve.

....

....

....

If you would like us to reply to you, please leave your contact details here.

Company: ....

Name: ....

Room number: ....

Signed: ....

Dept.Qual.Fair 06/08/1

In this unit
- customer feedback
- front office duties
- responding to problems
- checking guests out

Vocabulary

Front office duties

1 Match the pictures with the front office duties.

answer	FAQs
check	guests in
	guests out
control	access to the garage
deal with	overbookings
	cancellations
	requests for foreign exchange
	common problems
monitor	customer satisfaction
take	bookings
	messages for guests
	incoming phone calls
	final payment
update	guest histories

2 Which of these duties will a receptionist carry out

   1   before guests arrive?   3   when guests leave?

   2   during a guest's stay?

3 Which of the duties is the most routine?

4 Which of the duties would you find (a) the most pleasant, (b) the least pleasant?

Listening

Life in the front office

1 🎧 Erika works in a medium-sized hotel in the centre of Berlin. Listen to her talking about life in the hotel's front office. Which of the duties from *Vocabulary* does she mention, and in which order?

2 🎧 Listen again. Write T (true) or F (false).

   1   Erika has to spend all day dealing with emergencies.

   2   Taking messages for guests is a routine task in hotels.

   3   Answering questions is an opportunity to get to know your guests.

   4   It's impossible to predict what sorts of questions guests will ask you.

   5   Receptionists are responsible for monitoring customer satisfaction.

   6   A complaint is another name for a problem.

Find out

Work in pairs. Arrange a time with a receptionist in a local hotel. Go to the hotel and ask them about the different duties they carry out.

1 Find out which duties they

   1   have to carry out in the front office

   2   see as routine

   3   see as an opportunity to get to know their guests

   4   least like doing.

2 Ask them about common problems and about the procedure they are trained to follow when problems come up.

A study by Spain's Cantabria University showed that customers staying in luxury accommodation have higher expectations than those staying in 1-star hotels. As a result, feedback from customers in 4- and 5-star hotels is generally less positive.

15-minute, 24 hours a day satisfaction guarantee. Our staff are available around the clock ... If, however, your problem is not solved within fifteen minutes, we pick up the bill.
Ibis
Accor hotels

It's my job

Abdol Sadeghi

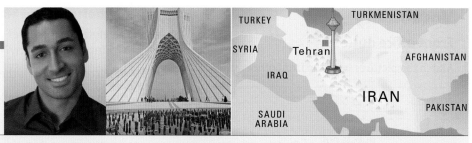

Many Westerners aren't sure, where Tehran is. But for 29-year-old Abdol Sadeghi, manager of the Tigran hotel complex, the Iranian capital is both his home and his place of work. Why did Abdol choose to work in the hotel trade? Which part of hotel work does he like best? What does he do in his free time? Read on and find out.

How long have you been in the hotel business?
I started very young – when I was twelve years old.

Why did you start so early?
My father believes that a good manager must know every part of the job. I started cleaning the toilets, working as

a waiter, and so on. He wanted me to try every aspect of the job, and not to start immediately as a manager.

Of course, you're not just a manager now?
No, I'm vice-president of our group, too.

What keeps you going?
I like my job. And it's a family business. It's what I can do to help my family.

And what do you enjoy most about your job?
Reception work, of course, because that puts me right in contact with the public.

An average day?
I don't think we have average days in our business. Most days I work twelve hours … but it depends on the day. Sometimes I work seventeen hours. But in the low season, I can usually get two days or three days off a week.

What do you do with that time?
Go out with friends, ski in winter, surf the Internet … visit my parents and my sister.

Just the sort of things anyone of his age does. Except for one thing. His mother and sister are in the Turkey branch of the business, and his father manages another complex in the north of Iran. Hotels run in the family!

Listening

Common problems

1 🎧 Look at the list of common problems. Listen to two people complaining to reception. In each case
   1 identify the problem from the list
   2 decide who should normally deal with it.

   a the receptionist   c the duty manager
   b another department

   1 air-conditioning does not work
   2 room too cold
   3 shower does not work
   4 not enough light in the bathroom
   5 noise from the street / other room
   6 TV image poor
   7 cannot connect to Internet
   8 cannot get the pay-TV channels
   9 room service slow
   10 non-smoking room smells of smoke

2 🎧 Listen again and decide if each receptionist has dealt with the problem effectively. If not, identify what they did wrong and say what should have happened. (Hint: remember what you learned in *Speaking* on p.43.)

3 Look at the other problems in the list. Work in groups and decide how they can best be dealt with. Report your decisions to the whole class.

● Language spot
Responding to problems

1 🎧 Listen to the situations again and complete the dialogues.

  1 **R** Oh, I'm very sorry about that. Would you like to change rooms?

     G Yes, I think I'd prefer that.

     R OK. I'll issue a new key right away and _____ you to change.

  2 **G** Until October! You're not serious? The weather forecast on TV said it would drop to 6° tonight.

     R I'll _____ you an extra blanket.

2 Which of the structures summarizes the way *get* is used in **1**?

  1 get something done
  2 get someone to do something
  3 get something for someone

3 Complete the dialogue using *get* and the words in brackets.

  G Hi. This is Room 431. It's very hot in my room.

  R I'm sorry about that, sir. Have you tried adjusting the thermostat?

  G Yes, I (the porter / adjust)[1] it as soon as we got into the room, but it's still very hot.

  R Mm. OK, I'll (maintenance / have a look)[2] at it.

  G Will it take long?

  R They're in the conference centre at the moment. I'll (them / do)[3] it as soon as they can.

  G Oh, OK. One more thing. Can we get tickets for the theatre tonight?

  R Of course. I'll (the concierge / reserve)[4] them for you.

4 Think of three more things you can get someone to do for a guest in a hotel. Tell your partner.

  EXAMPLE *You can get the bellboy to park a guest's car.*

➤➤ Go to **Grammar reference** p.127

Pronunciation

It's not easy to understand people who speak English quickly.

1 🎧 Listen. How many words are there in each sentence?

2 🎧 Work in pairs or threes. Listen again and write down the exact words for each sentence.

3 Which words were stressed most in each sentence? Mark each stressed word clearly.

4 Practise saying the sentences, paying special attention to the stressed syllables.

Speaking
Solving problems

Listen
↓
Apologize
↓
Act

1 Work in pairs. Student A, go to p.111. Student B, go to p.115. Act out the situations.

2 Act out new situations with the problems in the list on p.102, or make up problems of your own. The guest should call from their room.

What is it?

Reading

Check-out procedures

1 What do you know about check-out procedures in hotels? Share your experience and ideas with the class.

2 Look at the flow diagram for the check-out procedure. Which sections of the training manual correspond to 1–7 on the diagram?

3 Read the other sections of the manual. Work with a partner and try to draw the rest of the flow diagram.

4 Read these statements. Write T (true) or F (False).

1 Always check all items on a bill with the corresponding departments.

2 Hotel services used the night before departure will not appear on the front office screen.

3 With bills on credit through companies, do not show the client the bill.

4 Give all bills on credit through companies to the head receptionist.

5 With direct payment, explain each item on the bill verbally.

6 If you modify a bill, get the client to check it again.

FAIRMONT HOTEL
DURBAN

FRONT OFFICE PROCEDURES

Code: Chk. 02
Process: Check-in & Check-out
Revision: 1
Sub process: Check-out
Date: 27/04/20—

Process 4 – check-out
Check-out should follow the flow chart below.

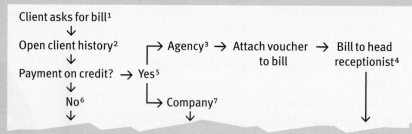

4.1 REQUEST FOR BILL

a The check-out process begins when a client asks for their bill. Bring up all of the documents connected to the client's room.

b Check the payment details on the screen. For payment on credit, go to 4.2. For direct payment, go to 4.3.

c Ask the client if they used any hotel services (bar, minibar, etc.) the previous evening. If they did, locate the charges on the computer and include them in the bill.

4.2 BILLS ISSUED TO CREDIT

4.2.1 Payment on credit through agencies

a Agency here means any travel agency, conference organizing agency, internet agency, or similar.

b Never show the bill to the client, in order to maintain the privacy of the data on it. All agency bills are given over to the head receptionist, who sends them to the agency.

4.2.2 Payment on credit to companies

a With company bills, always show the client the bill, unless there is an explicit order not to from the company. Ask the client to check the bill and sign it if correct.

b If the client is not happy with the bill, check all items with the corresponding departments. Modify the bill in the case of error. After making any modifications, ask the client to check the bill again, and sign it to show conformity.

4.3 DIRECT PAYMENT OF BILL

a Where a client has to make direct payment to Reception, in cash or with a credit card, the receptionist asks the client which method they will use.

b Show the client the bill, detailing each item verbally. If the client is happy with the bill, ask them to sign it to show conformity.

c If the client is not happy with the bill, check all items with the corresponding departments. Modify the bill in the case of error. Ask the client to check the bill again, and sign it to show conformity.

d Once conformity has been obtained, charge the client.

4.4 CUSTOMER SATISFACTION

On a daily basis, hand out customer satisfaction feedback forms at random to four or five clients, as described in Procedure P.Qual.06.

Listening

Can I have my bill?

1 🎧 Listen to a receptionist checking a client out.

  1 What is the client's name?

  2 How does the client pay?

  3 Is the bill correct?

2 🎧 Listen again. The receptionist makes a mistake with the correct check-out procedure. What is it?

3 What does the receptionist say to close the check-out procedure? What other things could you say just before a client leaves?

4 🎧 Look at the phrases below. Listen again. Which phrases does the receptionist use, and in which order?

  1 Could I just have your card for a moment?

  2 I'm just printing your bill out. Has everything been to your satisfaction?

  3 So, if I could just ask you to sign here.

  4 Did you have anything from the minibar last night?

  5 Here's your bill. Can I just ask you to check it?

  6 I'm sorry. I'll just check the bill again.

  7 I'm sorry. That was our mistake. I'll just print out the bill again for you.

  8 It's been a pleasure having you here.

  9 Here's your credit card and this is your copy of the payment slip.

  10 Will the bill be on the company account?

  11 Will you be paying by credit card?

5 Work in pairs. Which of the phrases in **4** would a receptionist use in each of these situations?

  1 A guest checking out and paying directly. The bill is correct.

  2 A guest checking out through a company account. There is a mistake in the bill.

Speaking

Checking guests out

Work in pairs. Role-play checking out, using the hotel bill.

1 Student A, you are the receptionist. Student B, you are the guest. Ask for your bill. Pay by credit card. The bill is correct.

2 Change roles. Student A, you are the guest. Ask for your bill. Pay through the company account. The bill is not correct.

3 Invent new situations. Decide how you are paying and if the bill is correct. Act out the situations.

Invoice Nº 47660	Room 302	Nº of people 1	Check in 08-07-20—	Check out 11-07-20—
Date	**Item**		**Due**	**Balance**
08-07-20—	Room		115.00	115.00
08-07-20—	Garage		15.00	130.00
09-07-20—	Breakfast		10.00	140.00
09-07-20—	Internet		07.50	147.50
09-07-20—	TV		08.50	156.00
09-07-20—	Room		115.00	271.00
09-07-20—	Garage		15.00	286.00
10-07-20—	Breakfast		10.00	296.00
10-07-20—	Sauna		30.00	326.00
10-07-20—	Restaurant		42.90	368.90
10-07-20—	Minibar		11.60	380.50
10-07-20—	Room		115.00	495.50
10-07-20—	Garage		15.00	510.50
11-07-20—	Breakfast		10.00	520.50
	Government tax – 12.5%			65.06
	Local tax – 2.5%			13.01
	Total taxes			78.07
	Balance due			**598.57**

Payment

Client's signature   Cardholder's signature

Total Quality Management (or TQM): a system of management that considers that every employee in the organization is responsible for keeping the highest standards of work in every aspect of the company's work in order to meet the needs of the customers
Oxford Business English Dictionary

loads of (n) a lot of

overall (adv) including everything or everyone; in total

Customer care
Quality standards

Many tourism organizations set 'quality standards' or 'performance standards' for their employees. Quality standards for checking out customers at a hotel might include the following.

- To smile and be courteous to the guest at all times.
- To use the guest's name when addressing him or her.
- To process a guest's closing account quickly and efficiently.
- To check all items are included in the bill and to agree them with the guest.
- To check the guest was happy with the service provided and, if not, to note any problems and pass them on to the management.

1 Look back at the reading on check-out procedures on p.104 and add one more quality standard.

2 Write three quality standards for greeting and checking in a guest at a hotel.

3 Choose another job in tourism – one that you might do in the future. Write three quality standards.

Reading
Unsolicited feedback

Hotels have mechanisms for getting feedback, but travellers sometimes put their opinions on websites. The opinions below are about a beach hotel in Minorca, Spain.

1 Work in pairs. Read the postings and summarize the feedback in the table by grading the opinions from 1 (very poor) to 5 (excellent).

Reviewer Hotel feature	1	2	3	4	5
Value for money					
Suitability for families					
Food					
Entertainment					
Staff					

2 Read the postings again and decide which
1 of the three postings is most positive
2 hotel features are criticized most strongly.

3 Make notes about any especially useful comments.

4 Work individually. Student A, go to p.115. Student B, go to p.116. Read the posting on your page. In your own words tell your partner what you found. Your partner will include it in the table.

1

We stayed at the Hotel Espiga D'Or in September with our four-year-old son and seven-year-old daughter. The hotel is right on the coast and 200 metres from the beach. The entertainment programme for children was superb. The staff were well-trained, creative, and energetic. The same staff also did the adult programme, which had a couple of really good shows. The only thing we found unpleasant was the smoking. Smoking is allowed in far too many places in our opinion! **Overall**, very good value for money.

2

We stayed at this hotel in September. When we booked, we knew it was really for families with young kids. Certainly the hotel was full of them while we were there, and they were quite noisy. But the hotel has a quiet adult pool area around the back, so if you like a bit of quiet sunbathing then that's the place to go. The food in the main restaurant was OK, though not much imagination went into it. We still had a good time and made some good friends. Oh, the staff – brilliant! And overall, excellent value for money.

Checklist

Assess your progress in this unit. Tick (✓) the statements which are true.

- [ ] I can understand somebody talking about front office duties
- [ ] I can respond to common hotel guest problems effectively
- [ ] I can understand the check-out procedure in a training manual
- [ ] I can check a hotel guest out following standard procedures
- [ ] I can write a short report summarizing feedback on hotel services

Writing
Reporting to the manager

Unsolicited feedback on Smithson package holidays

Hans Borgmann & Leena Kjisk
10 October 20—

Unsolicited feedback like the comments in *Reading* is important to hotels and to resort managers.

1 Work with a partner. You were holiday reps together in the Hotel Espiga D'Or. You are going to prepare a report for your Resort Manager about what you found on the Internet. Decide

- what information you are going to put in the report
- how many different sections your report will have
- if you are going to use tables and bullet points
- who will be responsible for writing each section.

2 Go to p.52 in the Writing Bank if you want to see a similar report.

3 Work individually and write the sections that you are responsible for. When you have finished, give them to your partner for checking.

4 Work together and prepare the final version of the report.

3

My husband and I stayed at the Hotel Espiga D'Or for two weeks last August with our kids. We had a fantastic time. The food was great. We loved the local food, and there were the usual pizzas and burgers for the kids. The entertainment was also excellent. **Loads of** really imaginative kids stuff – the hotel is more for families than couples. But as parents, we made some really good friends and had some great laughs. And all the staff were very polite and friendly, and spoke excellent English. Overall, very good value for money.

Key words

Nouns	Verbs
account	check someone out
agency	deal with
bill	sign
check-out process	update
cleanliness	
complaint	
conformity	
credit	
customer satisfaction	
direct payment	
feedback	
foreign exchange	
item	
overbookings	
payment slip	
routine task	
signature	
value for money	

Next stop

1 Tourism is a very complex industry. Which area in tourism would you like to go into – tour operation, travel agency work, the hotel trade, or tourist information?

2 What opportunities will you have in your chosen area to progress into tourism management?

3 What would you tell your employers about yourself if they asked you to justify your place on a junior management course?

Pairwork

Unit 2 p.15
Registering new arrivals

Student A

1 You are the guest. Use this information to register.

Room type: single
Number of nights: 6
Smoking / Non-smoking: Smoking
Other preferences: inside room / near lift
Garage: Yes
Payment: credit card

If you can, use your own ID and credit card during the check-in process.

2 Now change roles. You are the receptionist. Welcome the guest and complete the check-in screen.

Unit 5 p.43
I'm *very* sorry

Student A

You are a waiter. Familiarize yourself with these phrases before acting out your situations.

Checking satisfaction	*How are we doing? Is everything OK?*

Apologizing	
Basic	*I'm sorry.*
Stronger	*I'm so sorry.*
	I'm very sorry

Promising action	
food not hot	*I'll ask the chef to warm it up.*
glass / cutlery dirty	*I'll change it immediately.*
meat underdone	*I'll ask the chef to cook it some more.*
you've brought the wrong dish	*It's my mistake. I'll take it back to the kitchen.*
you've forgotten the water	*I'll get you some immediately.*
client unhappy with a dish	*Would you like me to get you something different?*
wait a long time to order / for bill	*We're very busy tonight. I'll get to you as soon as I can.*

Note: In difficult situations, add the phrase *I do apologize* after promising action.

REMEMBER! Stay calm. Show concern. Listen. Apologize. Clarify (if necessary). Promise action.

Unit 6 p.51
Giving information about the weather

Student A

Day	Weather	Wind	Other info
Tuesday		a little bit windy	possibly some showers
Wednesday		—	very hot in the afternoon
Thursday		quite windy	cold at night
Friday		—	probably rain by midday

Unit 10 p.87
Four specialized tours

Student A

Adventure sports – diving
Diving in the tropical waters of the Indian Ocean around the Maldives. Diving takes place every day, and all levels from beginners to advanced are catered for.

Experienced divers can also train as diving instructors.

Other extreme diving destinations include the Arctic region of northern Russia for ice-diving (diving under the ice).

Medical tourism
Going to another country for medical treatment, perhaps because the cost is cheaper or the service better and quicker.

Treatments can include fairly major operations, but cosmetic surgery and treatments are more common – facelifts, botox injections to forehead and eyes (to reduce appearance of ageing), collagen injections to lips, liposuction.

Most tourists coming for cosmetic surgery combine the trip with a relaxing holiday, so warm countries with good beaches are very popular destinations, in particular South Africa and Malaysia.

Unit 8 p.73
Checking the schedule

Student A

You are the tour guide. Phone the hotel to check the following.

Arrive 13.00 (later than booked)
Non-smoking section
16 pax
2 vegetarian
No children

Now you are the driver. This is the schedule you have.
08.00 Pick up at hotel
10.30 Comfort break
12.30 Arrive Melrose (lunch & tour)
14.00 Depart Melrose
17.00 Arrive Edinburgh
Hotel = Crown Hotel

Unit 9 p.81
Getting kids to make things

Student A

Materials
an A4-sized piece of black cardboard
a stapler
a white crayon
string
elastic
scissors

Instructions
Place the cardboard over the face, and use a crayon to mark the position of the eyes.
Carefully cut eyeholes in the position marked for each eye.
Use the crayon to colour the mask.
Make cuts in the cardboard, then fold it and staple it to give the mask volume.
Staple the elastic to the sides.
To make the hair, cut pieces of string of different lengths.
Make holes around the top of the mask. Next, pass a piece of string through each hole and tie a knot.
Do this until there is enough hair.

Unit 6 p.47
Receiving campers

Student A

Situation 1
You are the receptionist. Welcome the camper and complete the registration screen.

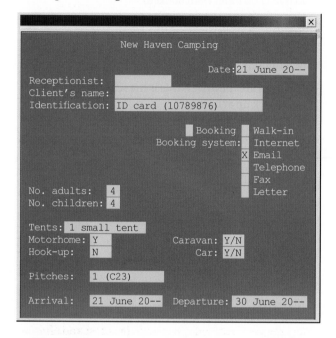

```
                                                    ×
              New Haven Camping

                            Date: 21 June 20--
   Receptionist:
   Client's name:
   Identification: ID card (10789876)

                              Booking     Walk-in
                   Booking system:        Internet
                                     X    Email
                                          Telephone
                                          Fax
   No. adults:     4                      Letter
   No. children:   4

   Tents:  1 small tent
   Motorhome:  Y            Caravan:  Y/N
   Hook-up:    N                Car:  Y/N

   Pitches:    1 (C23)

   Arrival:    21 June 20--  Departure: 30 June 20--
```

Situation 2
You are the camper. Use the information and book into the campsite.

Name: give your own name or invent a name.
Booking: no
Identification: passport K987630G
No. in group: 3 adults, 1 teenager (aged 15 – check this is still child rate)
No. of pitches: 1 pitch for 1 frame tent and 1 small tent.
Car: two
Stay: 9 days
Electricity: no
Facilities: check that there is a laundry

Unit 4 p.29
A day in the life of . . .

Student A

You are a transfer rep.

Location: Major destinations around the world, but especially the Mediterranean and the Caribbean.

Work: As a transfer rep, you accompany holidaymakers to and from the airport. During coach trips to the hotel you will be responsible for a simple welcome talk.

Main responsibilities
- Accompanying guests on day and night excursions
- Answering customers' questions and resolving complaints
- Basic resort administration
- Dealing with problems of overbooking at hotels
- Keeping guests occupied at the airport if there are any outgoing delays
- Making sure that the guests are booked into their accommodation
- Transferring customers to and from the airport

Unit 5 p.43
I'm *very* sorry

Student B

You are the customer. When the waiter asks you if everything is OK, complain about something.

I'm afraid that …	*I don't really like this dish.*
	my food isn't really that hot.
	the meat is a little underdone.
	this glass is dirty.
	this isn't what I ordered.
	we didn't get our water.
I'm sorry, but …	*we've been waiting for ages to order.*
	we've been waiting for ages for our bill.

Unit 9 p.81
Getting kids to make things

Student B

Materials
a large sheet of wrapping paper per group
crayons or coloured pencils
scissors
Blu-tack

Instructions
Lay out the paper on the floor.
One child from the group puts his / her hands on the paper.
The other children draw around the hands with crayons.
Once the outline has been made, another child puts his / her hands on the paper.
When all the children have hand outlines, the group can decorate the paper.
Use Blu-tack to stick the decorated paper on the wall for parents to see.

Alternatively, children can cut out their own hand shapes and decorate them.

Once they have decorated them, stick the shapes on a window.

Unit 12 p.103
Solving problems

Student A

Situation 1
You are the guest. Use the information and ring reception to complain. (You don't have to tell them all of the information at once.)

You are in Room 428. There is a lot of noise from the room below and you can't get to sleep. You know it's only 10.30 p.m., but you have a very early flight to catch in the morning. It sounds like the TV is on too loud, but it could be people arguing.

Situation 2
You are the receptionist. Listen to the guest and offer to solve their problem.

Situation 3
You are the guest. Use the information and ring reception to complain. (You don't have to tell them all of the information at once.)

Your shower does not work. The water is either very hot or very cold. You need a shower before you go out for supper. It's 7.00 p.m. and your table in the restaurant is booked for 8.30 p.m.

Situation 4
You are the receptionist. Listen to the guest and offer to solve their problem.

Unit 7 p.65
Three festivals

Student A

Dia de La Tradicion (Day of the Gaucho), Argentina

Introduction
Popular cultural event in ranch areas of Argentina
Takes place in grasslands 600 km south of Buenos Aires. Main centre = Santiago del Areco (more horses than cars)
Horse parades, dance, song, barbecue

History
Gaucho (= Argentine cowboy) – national cultural symbol
Mid-19th century – gaucho skills essential for agriculture (cattle – vital part of Argentine economy)
Gaucho folk dances (*milonga* and *payada*) contributed to more famous tango.

What happens
Takes place over two weekends – leading to 10 November
Displays of horsemanship, horse racing, parades of gauchos
Folk dances, climax on final Sunday
Barbecues – delicious beef / steaks – the best in the world

Unit 4 p.29
A day in the life of ...

Student B

You are a campsite rep.

Location: Campsites in Southern Europe and North America.

Work: Same as a family rep. In addition, you have to put up tents (montage) and take them down (de-montage). If the campsite has cabins, you have to clean these for new guests.

Main responsibilities
- Airport transfers
- Answering customers' questions and resolving complaints
- Basic resort administration
- Cleaning cabins
- Guiding excursions
- Montage & de-montage of tents
- Welcome meetings / selling excursions

Unit 6 p.51
Giving information about the weather

Student B

Day	Weather	Wind	Other info
Thursday	○	—	possibly some mist in the valleys
Friday	☁	a little bit windy	probably rain by the evening
Saturday	⛈	very windy	going to rain all day
Sunday	☁	—	some heavy showers

Unit 7 p.65
Three festivals

Student B

Sherry Festival in Jerez de la Frontera, Spain

Introduction
Autumn festival (September) – grape harvest celebration, horse shows, and flamenco dancing
Takes place in Andalusian town of Jerez
Diverse programme of entertainment

History
Centuries old celebration – exact origins unknown
Centres on Jerez, the most important of Spain's three sherry-producing towns – give thanks to the grape harvest

What happens
Start = parade of Queen of the Vintage – decorated with flowers, grapes, etc.
Masked courtiers throw sweets to children
Parade ends in Plaza de Arenal – drinking in sherry houses
Programme of parties, horse displays, concerts, flamenco dances
Special mass in church – blessing of the vines

Unit 11 p.98

Comparing conference centres

Student A

Name and location	The Westin Los Cabos, Mexico
Hotel facilities	Five-star hotel 243 guest rooms Good restaurants and bars, including La Cascada restaurant with a perfect view of the ocean
Conference rooms and facilities	Over 1,100 m² dedicated to meeting and conference facilities Seventeen meeting rooms – largest = 280 seats, smallest = 20 Internet service in all rooms Flexible room configurations allow for break-out rooms Complete audiovisual and production services
Other conference services	Videoconferencing services Dedicated conference organizer and audio-visual technician
Corporate hospitality	The Ballroom Under the Stars is one of the most popular private function rooms in the city. It offers views over the ocean and can provide hospitality for up to 450 people.
Other business services	Business centre with full secretarial services, boardroom, workstations, and business lounge
Extra events and activities	Sport fishing, golf, spa

Unit 7 p.64

Describing a festival

Festa del Redentore

Location:	Venice, Italy
Timing:	third weekend of July
Duration:	two days
Information:	www.comune.venezia.it/turismo

Introduction

↑ The Festa del Redentore – the Festival of the Redeemer – is a high point of the Venice summer. Thanks to a spectacular firework display the Redentore is a major tourist attraction.

History

↑ From 1575–77 ↑, Venice was hit by a terrible plague which killed more than a third of the city's inhabitants. In 1576, the city's leader, the Doge, promised to erect a church dedicated to the Redeemer, in return for help in ending the plague. On July 13, 1577, the plague was declared over, and work began to construct the church. It was also decided that Venice would forever give thanks on the third Sunday of July.

What happens

↑ From early on the Saturday, boats are decorated with flowers, lanterns, and balloons. St Mark's lagoon fills with as many as two thousand boats, ↑ their occupants eating and drinking as they wait for the traditional spectacular display of fireworks. (Arrangements can easily be made through your hotel for an evening with dinner on a boat.) At around 11.30 p.m. the display begins and the lagoon becomes one of the most atmospheric stages in the world, ↑ fireworks illuminating the spires, domes, and bell towers of the city.

On Sunday ↑ a pontoon of decorated gondolas and other boats is strung across the Giudecca canal ↑ to allow the faithful to walk to the church of the Redentore. The climax of the festival ↑ is the mass held in the presence of the Patriarch of Venice, ↑ a reminder that the Festa has a serious side. ↑

For more information visit the website quoted above.

Unit 11 p.98

Comparing conference centres

Student B

Name and location	The Mirage Hotel and Casino Resort, Las Vegas, USA
Hotel facilities	One of the world's finest luxury hotels – a South Seas oasis in one of the most bustling cities in the world
Conference rooms and facilities	15,800 m² convention complex, with spacious courtyards, foyers, and promenades for informal gatherings and meeting breaks. 26 meeting rooms, including an executive boardroom, a 3,700 m² pillar-less Grand Ballroom, and a 8,400 m² Events Centre. Conventions for up to 6,000 people. Ideal for trade shows and banquets. Audio-visual and communication equipment can be hired.
Other conference services	Photography and video services
Corporate hospitality	Casino and nightclub ideal for special corporate events
Other business services	Business Service Centre open daily: Equipment rental, courier services, fax, copying
Extra events and activities	Aquarium with dolphins. Spa and swimming pool. Betting, slot machines, and roulette, as well as the casino.

Unit 10 p.87

Four specialized tours

Student B

Life-seeing tourism

A term developed by Axel Dessau, Director of the Danish Tourism Board, to help tourists see not only the usual sights of a destination, but also to experience the real life of a place, particularly areas that they are interested in or that they work with in their own country.

For example, visitors might be government officials in their own country and might be interested in reviewing social problems and city government in the destination.

Expert guides will meet visitors and take them to visit city planning offices, schools, and social welfare centres. There may also be some special seminars arranged.

Denmark is one of the main destinations for this niche.

Genealogy tourism

Customers try to find out about their family history and write their family tree by researching records going back hundreds of years (in libraries and town halls). They also visit the locations where their ancestors lived and try to understand the way of life that their ancestors experienced.

Customers are typically people whose families emigrated from countries like Ireland or Scotland to live in the USA, Canada, Australia, New Zealand, or South Africa.

Unit 8 p.73

Checking the schedule

Student B

You are the receptionist at the hotel. This is the information you have.

Arrive 12.30
Non-smoking section
18 pax
No vegetarian meals booked
No children / high chairs

Now you are the tour guide. Phone tomorrow's driver to check the following.

07.30 Pick up (earlier than booked)
10.00 Comfort break (motorway)
12.00 Arrive Melrose (tour then lunch)
14.00 Depart Melrose
17.00 Arrive Edinburgh
Hotel = Crown Hotel for pax, but driver in Castle Inn

Unit 6 p.47

Receiving campers

Student B

Situation 1
You are the camper. Use the information and book into the campsite. Make sure you get what you booked.

Name: give your own name or invent a name.
Booking: made by email three months ago. You have the emails.
Identification: ID card (10789876)
No. in group: 4 adults, 3 children
No. of pitches: 1 pitch for motorhome, 1 pitch for frame tent
Stay: 9 days
Electricity: in one of the pitches.
Facilities: check that there is a shop and a swimming pool.

Situation 2
You are the receptionist. Complete the registration screen for the camper

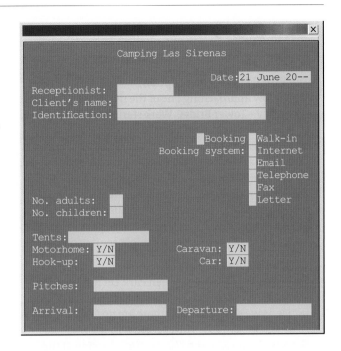

Unit 12 p.106

Unsolicited feedback

Student A

My stay in this hotel took place in August.
This is the first time we have been on a fully inclusive holiday. We weren't sure what that would mean in practice, but I have to say that we weren't disappointed. The food, for a start, was great – breakfast, snacks, lunch, dinner – all really great. The rooms were fine, too, very clean as was the whole hotel in general. Then the staff. Nothing was too much trouble for the hotel staff. The hotel entertainers were excellent. My seven-year-old daughter thought the Club de Piratas was amazing. We hardly saw her during the day, which was great for us and great for her. The disco for the adults was a must and after a couple of nights everybody knew all the words even of the Spanish songs. That was really fun. We did feel that the pools were too small for a hotel this size but we liked the adult pool by the bar, and the hotel was close to the beach, so often we just went there to swim.

I would recommend this hotel for families with young children or families with teenagers.

Unit 12 p.103

Solving problems

Student B

Situation 1
You are the receptionist. Listen to the guest and offer to solve their problem.

Situation 2
You are the guest. Use the information and ring reception to complain. (You don't have to tell them all of the information at once.)

You can't open the door with your key card. You are in Room 353. The card worked perfectly in the morning before you went out of the hotel.

Situation 3
You are the receptionist. Listen to the guest and offer to solve their problem.

Situation 4
You are the guest. Use the information and ring reception to complain. (You don't have to tell them all of the information at once.)

You asked for a snack from Room Service over 30 minutes ago. You tried ringing them again, but they are not answering the phone or it's engaged.

Unit 8 p.73

Preparing notes for commentaries

Top Visual Priority (description)

We're now approaching one of the most famous sights in the city – Tower Bridge. Work started on the bridge in 1886 and it took eight years to complete. It was regarded as one of the great engineering achievements of the day, and was the world's largest hydraulic bridge. The two towers are each 40 metres high, and the walkway is 45 metres above the river. The walkway was closed to the public in 1910 because there had been too many suicides. The bridge usually opens at least once a day, so if we're lucky, we might see it in operation!

Must tell (story / anecdote)

On your left, you can see Green Park. Let me tell you a story about why Green Park is called Green Park. You'll notice as we drive past that there are no flowers, just trees and grass – so it's just green. Why are there no flowers? Because in the 17th century, the king at the time used to walk through the park and pick flowers to take to his mistress – or girlfriend – who lived across the park. His wife, the queen, was, not surprisingly, not very happy about this and arranged for all the flowers to be taken out. Taking a bunch of grass to your girlfriend is not so romantic!

Unit 2 p.15

Registering new arrivals

Student B

1 You are the receptionist. Welcome the guest and complete the check-in screen.

2 Now change roles. You are the guest. Use this information to register.

Room type: double and twin
Number of nights: 3
Smoking / Non-smoking: Double = smoking; twin = non-smoking
Other preferences: outside rooms, preferably next to each other and not near the lift
Garage: Yes
Payment: credit card

If you can, use your own ID and credit card during the check-in process.

Unit 12 p.106

Unsolicited feedback

Student B

My stay in this hotel took place in June.

We had a very nice fortnight at this hotel in June this year. In fact, this visit was our second time and we are thinking of booking for next year! The room was clean but basic, which we knew it would be, but it has a fantastic view of the sea. We enjoyed the meals again this year. We're not keen on foreign food, so not everything was to our individual tastes, but there was always plenty of it, so neither of us ever went hungry. The adults-only dining area was a lovely new idea. Children are a lot of fun, but it is nice to be able to escape to an adult environment from time to time. We couldn't always get two sunbeds together. There seemed to be fewer sunbeds this year. Strange. In the end we decided to hire a car. They're so cheap here. And of course, there are plenty of nice beaches within easy reach. All in all a nice resort and a nice hotel with really friendly and helpful staff and well worth another return visit or two.

I would recommend this hotel for families with young children (and oldies like us, too).

```
                    C H E C K - I N
Reservation number: WALK-IN
Rm type:                    Terms:
No. rms:                    Rate:   FULL
---------------------------------------------------
Arrive:   10.10.08          ETA:
Nights:
Depart:                     Pre-asig. rm(s):
---------------------------------------------------
Name:                       Initials:         VIP: --
Address:                    Tel:
                            Email:
Nationality:                ID:     --
Guest 2: --
Guest 3: --                 Garage: --
---------------------------------------------------
Deposit:                    Due: --      Received: --
Reservation by:                  Payment:
Voucher/Credit card no.:
---------------------------------------------------
Comments:
---------------------------------------------------
   [F2-Guest history]  [F7-print]  [F8-Arrivals]
```

Unit 7 p.65

Three festivals

Student C

Songkran Water Festival, Thailand

Introduction

Buddhist New Year Festival – 4 days – mid-April – all over Thailand, Laos, Burma, south-west China – main centre = Chiang Mai, north Thailand
Based on water: water-fights, water-throwing, bathing, fountains

History

Celebrated for hundreds of years
Thanksgiving for New Year – a new beginning – a time to think back over the past year – wash away sins and bad luck
A time for families to get together

What happens

Day 1: Houses cleaned – procession of Buddha images and floats – water thrown over procession – colourful flags, paper lanterns
Day 2: Special food cooked – sand collected from rivers to make towers in temple courtyards
Day 3: first day of new year – water fights start – food and new robes given to monks
Day 4: people visit and pay respect to ancestors – pour scented water over hands

Unit 11 p.98

Comparing conference centres

Student C

Name and location	The Hotel at Chelsea, located at Stamford Bridge, home of Chelsea Football Club, London, UK
Hotel facilities	275 bedroom, 4-star hotel Five restaurants and bars Spa, health club, and 25-metre swimming pool
Conference rooms and facilities	Purpose-built suites can accommodate 600 for a reception and 280 for a conference. Natural light and views of the famous football pitch. Great Hall can accommodate 800 in theatre-style. Modern audio-visual equipment
Other conference services	Variety of smaller meeting rooms Match-day hospitality – see corporate hospitality
Corporate hospitality	Corporate events in executive boxes on match-day, includes: reserved seats, pre-match three-course meal, complimentary bar, half-time and full-time refreshments, exclusive Chelsea gift, and celebrity guest speaker
Other business services	Full range of business services Four boardroom-style meeting rooms
Extra events and activities	Match-day packages, including overnight stay Stadium tours

Grammar reference

1 Greeting and introducing

We can use several ways to greet people or to introduce ourselves.

Greeting

Informal

Hello / Hi, Julia – it's nice to see you again.

Formal

Good morning / afternoon / evening, Mrs Yashimoto. Here's your room key.

Welcoming

Welcome. / Welcome to Toronto.

NOT *Welcome at Toronto.*

Or, if returning to a place:

Welcome back to Toronto.

Introducing yourself

Informal

Hi. My name's Johann.
Oh, hi. I'm Alex.

Formal

Good evening. My name is Mr Elliott.
May I introduce myself? I'm a colleague of Ms Pierron.

Introducing someone else

This is …
Have you met … ?

Note that we only use *that's* or *that is* to identify someone who is not standing nearby.

You see the tall man with the glasses standing over there? That's Dr Mashiko.

When we introduce more than one person, we usually do so individually.

This is Ms Fleischman and this is Professor Schwartz.

NOT *These are Ms Fleischman and Professor Schwartz.*

Checking someone's identity

You must be …

As well as using *must* for obligation (*You must pay for the ticket*), we also use it when we are quite certain about something. Remember that *must* is always followed by infinitive without *to*.

We use *You must be* to refer to one or more people.

You must be the tour guide.
You must be Mr and Mrs Jakobsen.

It's …, isn't it?

This is only used when addressing one person, and does not change. It is usually used with someone whose name we think we already know.

Hi. It's David, isn't it?

NOT *You're …, aren't you?*

Making an offer

As well as using *can* for ability, requests, and permission, we can also use it to make an offer.

Can I / we + get / give / offer, etc.

Can I get you some more wine?
Can we do anything to help?

Note that the correct response is *Yes / No, thank you.* It is not polite to say *Yes, you can.*

2 Where things are

We can use several prepositions and phrases to describe where a person or thing is located.

in   enclosed spaces, e.g. rooms, buildings, furniture
in the basement
in the hotel
in the corner

         limited areas, e.g. towns, parks, countries, continents
in the hotel forecourt
in America

at   general location, i.e. it is not important whether something or someone is inside or outside a building
Mr Hamer called to say that he is already at the airport.

         a specific point or feature in the room
I'll wait for you at the meeting point.

         in expressions such as *at the end (of)*
Go down this corridor, and you'll find the gym at the end.
You'll find the gym at the end of the corridor.

on surfaces, e.g. walls, floors, shelves
on *the first floor*
on *the roof*
on *the left / right*
*Turn left and the hairdresser's is **on** the right.*
NOT ~~in the left~~

We use both **next to** and **near** to talk about how close things or people are, but *next to* means that one thing or person is at the side of another, while *near* tells us only that one thing or person is not far away from another.
*Is the garage **next to** the hotel? – No, but it's very **near**.*

Between means having someone or something on each side.
*The toilets are located **between** the restaurant and the bar.*

Opposite means that one thing or person is facing another.
*You'll see the lifts immediately – they're **opposite** the main entrance.*

Over there is similar to *there*, but indicates a longer distance away from ourselves. We can combine *over there* with other prepositions to describe more accurately where something is.
*Don't use that lift. Use the one **over there**.*
*The business corner is **over there next to** the lounge.*

3 Giving directions and prepositions of movement, Recommending and promoting

Giving directions

When giving directions, we usually use the imperative form of the verb. This is the same as the infinitive:
Go … , Take … , Turn … .

However, we can also use an *if* sentence, as follows.

If you take the first road on the left, **you'll see** the market on the right.

= *If* + *you* + infinitive without *to*, *you* + *will (you'll)* + infinitive without *to*

Prepositions of movement

Although some of the verbs we use when giving directions are not followed by a preposition, e.g. *reach*, it is common for many verbs to combine with one preposition or more.

These verbs include *come, get*, and *go*.

They combine with prepositions such as *along, at, down, out of, past, through*, and *up*.

The same verb may be followed by different prepositions to give different meanings.
come out of = leave
come to = reach

On the other hand, different verb + preposition combinations can sometimes have the same meaning. One of the commonest verbs to use when giving directions is *Go*, but there are alternatives such as *Head* and *Walk*.

***Go / Head / Walk** past the station, then turn left.*
***Go / Head / Walk** along here for about five minutes.*

Note that the prepositions *down* and *up* do not necessarily mean that the route is up or down a hill. When combined with *go*, etc., these two prepositions have a similar meaning to *along*.

*Go **down** this road.*
*Head **up** the High Street until you reach the bank.*

out of (= leaving a location) and *at* (= reaching a fixed point) can combine with a number of verbs.
*When you **come out of** the market, turn left.*
***Turn right at** the Tourist Information Centre.*

cut combines with *through* to indicate a shorter route.
*The best way to get to the main road is to **cut through** the park.*

Do not confuse *towards* and *to*. *Towards* means 'in the direction of', whereas *to* means 'as far as'.
*Walk **towards** the church but turn left before you reach it.*
*Walk **to** the church and cut through the churchyard.*

Recommending and promoting

In tourism texts you'll find several ways to make a recommendation or promotion.

negative + *without*

No visit / trip / journey is complete without + -ing form or noun
No *trip* **is complete without** *visiting / a visit to the museum.*

or

Don't + infinitive without to (+ place name) + without + -ing form
Don't *leave (Liverpool)* **without** *visiting the museum.*

well worth

(well) **worth** *+ -ing* form / noun
The Cavern Club is **worth** *visiting / a visit.*

Well worth + -ing form offers a stronger recommendation than *worth + -ing* form.

Why not

Why not + infinitive without to
Why not watch a football match?

If sentences

If + clause + **you could** *+ infinitive without to*
If you want to get out and about, **you could** *start at Pleasureland.*

We can also use *If* with *why not ...?*
If you like shopping, **why not** *go along to Albert Dock?*

a must

We only use *must* as a noun when we are recommending or promoting a place.
The Beatles Museum is **a must** *for any fans of the Fab Four.*

The following expressions are used more in promotional texts.

You can find

In Liverpool, **you can find** *everything you need for a fantastic holiday.*

Whether

Whether is used to give more than one option.
Whether *you're interested in music or art, football or shopping, Liverpool meets all your expectations.*

... boast ...

We use *boast* to talk about an attraction that we would like to promote.
The city centre **boasts** *the biggest range of shops in the region.*

4 Advice and obligation

Advice

should

We use *should* and *shouldn't* to tell someone what we think is the best thing to do, or not to do.

Positive

You **should** make sure that you have a good night's sleep before changeover.

= subject + *should* + infinitive without *to*

Negative

You **shouldn't** get too drunk on your day off.

= subject + *shouldn't* + infinitive without *to*

avoid

We use *avoid* to mean the same as *You shouldn't.* However, *avoid* has a different form.

Avoid partying too much at the beginning of the season.

Avoid this if you can.

= *Avoid + -ing* form

= *Avoid* + noun or pronoun

Note that *avoid* can also be combined with *You should.*

You **should avoid** *partying too much.*

Don't

Don't is used when giving advice.

Don't expect to have a private life as a ski rep.

= *Don't* + infinitive without *to*

Note that we cannot say *You don't ...* when giving advice.

NOT *~~You don't expect to have a private life.~~*

Obligation

have to

We use *have to* to talk about an action that is necessary because of laws or rules.

> You **have to** wear your uniform at all times when on duty.

= subject + *have to* + infinitive without *to*

mustn't

mustn't is the negative form of *have to*. We use *mustn't* to tell someone what they can't do because of laws or rules.

> You **mustn't** drink alcohol before you go skiing. There's a fine of € 500.

= subject + *mustn't* + infinitive without *to*

5 Describing food, Relative clauses

Describing food

We use the Passive when we do not know who did something, or when it is not important to say who did it.

As with Active sentences, we can use different tenses in the Passive, e.g. Present Passive, Past Simple Passive, etc.

Present Passive

The Present Passive is often used to talk about a custom that exists in the present.

> A pasta dish **is served** before the main course.
>
> A special meal **is eaten** on Friday evening.

= subject + Present Simple of *be* + past participle

We also use the Present Passive to describe a process such as the method of making and preparing a dish, or talking about ingredients and accompaniments. In this case, we often use the prepositions *of* or *with* after the Passive verb.

*A salade Marocaine **is made of** chopped tomatoes.*
*Schnitzel **is served with** potato salad.*
*This dish **is cooked with** potatoes and carrots.*

Be careful to use the correct preposition after the verb.

It is possible to use other prepositions after the Passive, but these depend on the main verb.

*The meat **is covered in** breadcrumbs.*

Relative clauses – *who*, *which*, and *that*

We use relative clauses to connect two ideas. There are two types of relative clause.

Non-defining

Look at the following sentences.
I really love sushi. Sushi is our national dish.

By using the pronoun *who* or *which*, we can combine the two sentences and avoid repeating the subject.
*I really love sushi, **which** is our national dish.*
MAIN CLAUSE   RELATIVE CLAUSE

We use *which* to refer to a thing or things, and *who* to refer to a person or people.

In this way,

Turkish food is popular among tasters. Tasters visit regions as part of their holiday.

becomes

*Turkish food is popular among tasters, **who** visit regions as part of their holiday.*

Note that in the sentences containing *which* and *who*, the two parts of the sentence are separated by a comma. The second part of the sentence is called a non-defining relative clause. This is because what comes after the comma is simply additional information, which we do not need in order to understand the whole sentence.

Defining

The second type of relative clause also connects two ideas, but in a different way. Look at the following sentences.
A tagine is a pot. A tagine is used to cook food in.
*A tagine is a pot **which** is used to cook food in.*
MAIN CLAUSE   RELATIVE CLAUSE

Also

Tasters are tourists. Tasters are interested in the food of the region.
*Tasters are tourists **who** are interested in the food of the region.*
MAIN CLAUSE   RELATIVE CLAUSE

In this case, the relative clause is not just giving additional information, and does not come after a comma. Instead, it is an essential part of the sentence that helps us to identify which things or people we are talking about.

Note that in a defining relative clause, we can use *that* instead of *which* or *who*.

*A tagine is a pot **that** is used to cook food in.*
*Tasters are tourists **that** are interested in the food of the region.*

We cannot use *that* in non-defining relative clauses.

NOT *I really love sushi, that is our national dish.*

6 Making predictions

will

The most common way of making predictions is by using *will*.

Positive

The rain **will** last all day. It usually does.

= subject + *will* + infinitive without *to*

Negative

These strong winds **won't** die down today, I'm afraid.

= subject + *won't (will not)* + infinitive without *to*

Questions

Will the storms last all day?

= *Will* + subject + infinitive without *to*

However, because we are often uncertain about the likely outcome of a situation, it is common to use *will* in combination with the verb *think*.

*I **think** it **will** be overcast all day.*
*We **don't think** these heavy showers **will** last.*
*Do you **think** that the rain **will** clear soon?*

Note that we do not tend to use the positive form of *think* with *won't / will not*.

NOT *We think these heavy showers won't last.*

Other question forms when asking someone to make a prediction are

Do you know if the café **will be** open?

= *Do you know if* + subject + *will* + infinitive without *to*

and

Do you know what the food **will be like?**

= *Do you know what* + subject + *will be like*

It is more polite to use *Do you think …?* or *Do you know …?* when asking someone to make a prediction, as *will* is rather impolite.

going to

We use *going to* + infinitive without *to* to make a prediction based on what has already started to happen. For example, we could use *going to* to predict rainy or stormy weather if the sky has started to get darker.

Look at those clouds! It's **going to** rain.

= *going to* + infinitive without *to*

We also use *going to* when reporting a prediction made by someone else. If we are not talking about a specific person, we use the pronoun *they*.

*You should take a coat. They said it's **going to** get a bit colder this afternoon.*

7 The Passive

We use a Passive verb when we do not know who did something, or when it is not important to say who did it. While we can use the Passive to say something in a more formal way, it is used very commonly when we are describing buildings and attractions.

Present Passive

The Present Passive describes a scene, process, or situation that exists in the present.

The main hall **is used** for special occasions.

The gardens **are lit** at night.

= subject + Present Simple of *be* + past participle

If we put the two sentences above into an Active form, we would need to add a subject to say who was using the main hall and who lit the gardens at night.

***They** use the main hall for special occasions.*
***People** light the gardens at night.*

We use the Passive to avoid having to mention who performed the action if we think it is not relevant, or if we don't know who did it.

Past Passive

The Past Passive describes a finished action, rather than a situation that exists now.

The tower **was added in** 1654.

The walls of the city **were built** in the tenth century.

= subject + Past Simple of *be* + past participle

As for the Present Passive, if we used an Active verb form, we would need to add a subject.

Someone added the tower in 1654.

They built the walls of the city in the tenth century.

Passive with *by*, *of*, *for*

Note that it is common to use these prepositions to add more information after a Passive verb form.

by   We use *by* if we want to use a Passive verb form but also need to mention who made or did something.

*The Eiffel tower was built **by** Gustave Eiffel.*

of   We use *of* to describe the material that is used to make something.

*The building is made **of** stone.*

for   We use *for* + -*ing* form or noun to talk about the purpose of, or reason *for*, doing something.

*The Great Hall was built by the prince **for** entertaining guests.*

8 Explaining arrangements, Language of calming and dealing with a crisis

Explaining arrangements

There are several ways to talk about the future.

Present Simple

We can use the Present Simple to talk about a timetabled event.

The coach **departs** at 10.30 on Sundays.

We also use the Present Simple in a two-part sentence after *when*, *if*, *before*, *after*, *as soon as*, and *until*. The other part of the sentence uses *will*, *going to*, or the imperative.

*Please give me a call **as soon as** you **arrive** at the hotel.*
NOT *… as soon as you will arrive at the hotel.*

Present Continuous

We can also use the Present Continuous to talk about a pre-arranged event, but not one that is part of a regular programme or timetable.

The coach **is leaving** in five minutes.

We**'re** all **going** to the club tonight.

= subject + Present Simple of *be* + -*ing* form

NOT *The coach is leaving every Sunday at noon.*

It is very common to use a time expression with the Present Continuous when talking about the future, so that it is not confused with something that is happening now. Compare the following.

FUTURE   *The coach is leaving in five minutes.*

PRESENT   *The coach is leaving.*

will future

will is not normally used to talk about timetables or planned events. We use *will* when we decide what to do at that particular moment, e.g. to promise or offer to do something, and to make requests.

I**'ll wake** you up before we arrive.

subject + *will* ('*ll*) + infinitive without *to*

Future Continuous

We use the Future Continuous to talk about what will be happening at a certain point in the future.

During the journey, **we'll be offering** you a complimentary drink.

= subject + *will* + *be* + -*ing* form

going to future

We use *going to* + infinitive without *to* when we talk about our intentions. We have already decided what to do.

I**'m going to** read out your names to check that you're all here.

= subject + Present Simple of *be* + -*ing* form

going to is also used when we can see the result of something that is happening now.

*Take a coat. It'**s going to** be cold.*

Language of calming and dealing with a crisis

We can use several ways to reassure someone about a situation.

Imperative

Positive

> Please **keep** calm.
>
> **Calm** down.

= infinitive without *to* + adjective or adverb

Note that some verbs are followed by a preposition, e.g.

Try + to
Look + at

> **Try to** relax.
>
> **Look at** me.

= infinitive without *to* + preposition + infinitive without *to*

Negative

> **Don't worry.**
>
> Please **don't apologize.**

= Don't + infinitive without *to*

Let

The verb *let* means 'allow', and is used in the imperative form. It is followed by a name or object pronoun, e.g. *me, him, her.*

Positive

> **Let** me explain.
>
> Please **let** us help you.

= *Let* + object pronoun + infinitive without *to*

The negative form *Don't let* + object pronoun + infinitive without *to* exists, but is not used when calming a person down.

Let's

Note that we can use *Let's* as a means of suggesting a solution or course of action. This is not the same as the imperative *Let*, and has a different form.

> **Let's** go and ask at the desk.

= *Let's* + infinitive without *to*

going to

going to is another way to talk about a decision or course of action that we have made. We use *going to* when we have thought about the situation, and have come to a decision.

> This is what we**'re going to** do.

= *going to* + infinitive without *to*

will

We use *will* when we are offering to do something, or when we decide to do something immediately.

> I**'ll tell** you what I**'ll do.**

= subject + *will* ('ll) + infinitive without *to*

9 Indefinite pronouns, Helping kids to make things

Indefinite pronouns

We can combine *any, every, no,* and *some* with *-one / -body, -thing,* or *-where*. You must leave a space between *no* and *one*, but all other combinations form a single word. The meanings of the new words are easy to guess, for example

anyone / anybody = it doesn't matter who
everywhere = all the places
nothing = not one thing
someone / somebody = a person

We use *any* when we are talking generally, whereas *some* could refer to a particular person, thing, or place.

We use a singular verb with all these combinations.

Everyone has *breakfast in the same restaurant.*
Nothing is *wrong with the programme.*

After words with *-one* or *-body*, we normally use *they / them / their* to show possession, rather than *his / her / its.*

Everyone *is having* **their** *lunch.*

Generally, when *any-, every-, no-,* and *some-* are the subject of the sentence or clause, we use a positive verb.

No one has *complained.*
Anything is *possible on this tour!*
Make sure that **someone** *knows where you are going.*

NOT ~~No one hasn't complained.~~

When *any-* is the object of the sentence, the main verb is negative. It is also common to use *any-* in questions.

*I didn't like **anything** on the menu.*
*Did you learn **anything** on the course?*

When *no-* is the object of the sentence, the main verb is positive.

*I learnt **nothing** on the course.*

some is not commonly used in the negative or in questions, while *every-* can be used in the positive, negative, and in questions.

We can combine *something, everyone*, etc. with other adjectives.

***Did you go** anywhere interesting?*

Helping kids to make things

When giving instructions, we often use the imperative.

Positive

> **Inflate** one of the balloons.

= infinitive without *to*

Negative

> Don't **put** too much water in it.

= *Don't* + infinitive without *to*

In a series of instructions, we need to be able to say in what order things have to be done. One way to do this is to use words such as *now, then*, and *after that*.

***Now** get another balloon and fill it with water. **Then** tie a knot in it.*

Another way is to use *when* with either the Present Simple or Present Perfect. Be careful, as the tense you use changes the meaning of the sentence.

When + Present Simple

We use *when* with the Present Simple to describe two actions that happen at the same time.

***When** you **tie** the knot, make the shape of the balloon as round as possible.*

When + Present Perfect

We use *when* with the Present Perfect to talk about one action that follows another.

FIRST ACTION	SECOND ACTION

***When** you**'ve let** the air out, place the first balloon inside it.*

Remember that the form of the Present Perfect is subject + *have / has* + past participle.

Instead of *When* + Present Perfect, we can use *Once*.

***Once** you**'ve stretched** the balloon, fill it with water.*

10 Responding to special requests, Identifying and checking special needs

Responding to special requests

There are several expressions we can use when responding to requests. These carry different degrees of certainty, ranging from 'definitely yes' to 'definitely not'.

definitely yes	*Of course.* *No problem.*
probably yes	*That **shouldn't** be a problem.* *I don't see why not.*
possibly yes	*There **might** be a problem (if …).* *You **may** need to pay something.* *I'm not sure.* *We **may** possibly be able to make arrangements.*
definitely not	*Sorry, you **can't**.* *You **mustn't** remove them from their natural habitat.*

Note the use of modal verbs *shouldn't, can't, mustn't, may*, and *might* in the sentences above.

Form of modal verbs

All modal verbs are followed by infinitive without *to*. They do not have an *-s* in the third person singular, and do not use the auxiliary *do* to form the negative and questions.

Positive

> That **should** be all right.

= subject + *must / can / should / may / might* + infinitive without *to*

Negative

You **mustn't** remove them from their natural habitat.

= subject + *mustn't / can't / shouldn't / may not / mightn't* + infinitive without *to*

Note that in this form *may not* is never shortened to *mayn't*.

Questions

Can we take some of the plants back with us?

= *Must / Can / Should / May / Might* + subject + infinitive without *to*

Use of modal verbs

Should / shouldn't is often used when we are advising someone (not) to do something. When responding to a request, it generally means that an action may or may not be possible.

Might / mightn't is always used to talk about a small possibility of something happening.

May / may not is similar to *might / mightn't*, but suggests a stronger possibility.

Can / can't is used in many situations, e.g. to talk about ability, to ask for permission, and to make requests. When responding to a request, we use *can / can't* to say what someone is (not) permitted to do because of the circumstances.

Must / mustn't is a stronger way of telling someone that they can or can't do something, generally because there is a rule or law which requires or forbids it.

Identifying and checking special needs

We can use a Passive form when we want to check that arrangements have been made.

Present Passive

We can use the Present Simple to talk about a timetabled event.

Everything **is set up** for the guests.

= subject + Present Simple of *be* + past participle

Note that the past participle of many verbs is the same as the Past Simple form.

infinitive	Past Simple	past participle
call	*called*	*called*
buy	*bought*	*bought*

However, some verbs have a different past participle form, which must be learned.

give	*gave*	*given*

We can use the Passive in other tenses.

Present Continuous Passive

The hotel **is being upgraded**.

= subject + Present Simple of *be* + *-ing* form + past participle

Past Passive

A new extension **was added** last year.

= subject + Past Simple of *be* + past participle

Present Perfect Passive

The whole entrance **has been adapted**.

= subject + Present Perfect of *be* + past participle

need + to be + past participle

To talk about changes that are necessary we can use *need*. The most common way to do this is by using *need + to be*.

We **need to be accommodated** in ground floor rooms.

= subject + Present Simple of *need + to be* + past participle

need + -ing form

need + -ing form is more informal.

The bar **needs upgrading**.

= subject + Present Simple of *need + -ing* form

The forms *need + to be* and *need + -ing* form have a similar meaning when we talk about work that is necessary.

The bar **needs to be upgraded.**
The bar **needs upgrading.**

However, when we talk about people, we generally use *need + to be*.

N O T ~~We need accommodating in ground floor rooms.~~

Need can also be used in other tenses.
The group **will need to come** through reception.

11 Describing dimensions, capacity, and facilities

Describing dimensions, capacity, and facilities

We talk about dimensions in the following ways.

Present Simple of *measure*

The room **measures** 30 metres by 15 metres.

Noun + *be*

The **dimensions** of the room **are** 30 metres by 15 metres.

To talk about capacity, we use the following.

can

Can + infinitive without to is used to talk about many things but, when combined with the verb *seat*, refers specifically to the capacity of a room or other space.

The room **can seat** over 500 people.

Prepositions such as over and up to are frequently used when describing capacity.

Noun + *have / has a capacity of*

Both **rooms have a capacity of** up to 500 people.

To talk about facilities we use the following forms.

Present Passive

We can use the Present Passive of the verb *equip* + *with*.

The room **is equipped with** a projector.

= subject + Present Simple of be + past participle

Present Simple of *contain*

The room **contains** audio-visual equipment and a flip chart.

can

We use can + infinitive without to to talk about facilities when combined with a personal pronoun and a verb such as *provide* or *offer*.

We can provide a lamination service.

have / has got

The room **has got** videoconferencing facilities.

We **have got** a digital projector.

There is ('s) / There are

There's a laptop in each room.

12 Responding to problems

When responding to problems, we often use *will* or *can* + infinitive without to to tell someone what we are going to do.

I'll **ask** the engineer to look at your air-conditioning unit.

I can **ask** the housekeeper to dry-clean your coat.

get

Another common way to talk about helping someone is to use *get*. This is a very common verb in English, and has several different meanings. It is found in many phrasal verbs, e.g. *get out*, as well as in expressions such as *get into bed*. Some meanings are used more in speech, e.g.

get + an idea or joke = understand – I don't get it. Can you explain it again?

However, there are many other meanings of get that can be used in both written and spoken English.

have got = have – **Have** you **got** any luggage?

get (+ noun) = receive – I didn't **get** the message.

get to (+ noun) = arrive at / in – I **got** to the airport just in time.

get (+ adjective) = become – It's **getting** very warm.

get (+ noun) = obtain or buy – It's cold. I'll **get** an extra blanket.

When responding to problems, it often means 'obtain'.

To make it clear that we are doing something for another person, we generally add *for* + pronoun or noun.

I'll get an extra blanket **for you.**

I'll get some aspirin **for your wife.**

Note that another very common way of saying this is for the person, e.g. you, to follow get.

I'll **get you** an extra blanket.

I'll **get your wife** some aspirin.

get + object + infinitive with *to*

We use this structure when we promise to ask another person to help in some way.

I'll **get maintenance to look** *at the heating in your room.*

I'll **get the porter to help** *you.*

I'll **get the housekeeper to give** *you a blanket.*

Listening scripts

Unit 1 Listening

Greeting and introducing

1
Hello, Peter – it's great to see you again. Welcome to Atlanta. How was your flight?

2
Hello, and thank you for joining us tonight. My name's Praphat and this is my colleague, Amphai. We'll be looking after you on tonight's excursion.

3
Good evening, Mr Ellman. Is everything to your satisfaction? Can I get you some more wine?

4
May I introduce myself? My name is Chie Mashida and I'm the manager. I'd like to introduce you to the people who are going to be looking after you during the conference. This is Masako …

5
A Hi, it's Johann, isn't it? Glad you could make it. How are you doing?
B Good, yeah. You?
A Not bad. Have you met Lucy? She organized this reception.

6
Ladies and gentlemen, on behalf of Paradise Cruises, we'd like to welcome you all on board. We're pleased to offer you a complimentary glass of champagne.

7
You must be Ms Holweger. Welcome to Copenhagen. Let me take your bag for you.

8
Welcome back, Dr Allegretti. Nice to see you again. We've put you in your usual room.

Unit 1 Listening

Car hire dialogue

E= Employee, C = Customer

E Good afternoon, sir. Can I help you?
C Yes, hello. We pre-booked a car and we've come to pick it up.
E Certainly. What's your name?
C Jacobson.
E OK, was it an online booking?
C Yes, we booked it from the UK.
E Right. Here we are. You booked the four-door economy manual with air-conditioning?
C That's right.
E We've got a special offer at the moment. Would you like to upgrade to the compact four-door for just an extra ten rand a day?
C No, thanks. There's just the three of us. I think we'll be OK in the economy.
E OK. I just need to check a few things. You're going to drop off here in ten days' time. Is that correct?
C Correct. On the 21st of August.
E Can you confirm your age?
C I'm 26.
E And you've decided to stay with the four-door economy manual with air-conditioning?
C Yes.
E I notice you've only booked the collision damage waiver and the third-party liability. Do you want to take out any additional insurance cover?
C I did think about the windscreen cover, but I decided against it.
E OK. Do you want to book any extras?
C I thought we'd booked the baby seat?
E It's not here, but that's no problem, sir. We can easily add it. How old is the little one?
C She's two.
E Right, I'll add that to the invoice. Is there anything else you require?
C No, that's everything, thank you.
E OK, could you just sign here?
C Here? OK.
E How will you be paying the balance?
C By credit card. Here you are.
E Thank you … Right, Mr Jacobson, here's the key. This is my colleague, Evan. He'll bring the car round for you and show you the basics. And we'll see you in ten days' time. Have a great trip.
C Thank you.

Unit 1 Pronunciation

1	Chrysler	5	Mercedes
2	Citroën	6	Opel
3	Ford	7	Renault
4	Hyundai	8	Toyota

Unit 2 Listening

Registration procedures

R = Receptionist, G = Guest

a
R Good evening, Ms Meier. How nice to see you again.
G Good evening. It's nice to be back, even if it's for work.
R Well, if we didn't have a job to go to … I'm afraid your usual room isn't free, Ms Meier. But I can put you in 615. That's on the next floor and has the same view. Would that be all right?
G Yes, of course.

b
R Good evening, sir. How can we help you?
G Do you have a double room for tonight?
R Just one moment and I'll check availability. Would that be a non-smoking room, sir?
G Preferably.
R And just for the one night?
G Yes, just for tonight.
R Yes, we can do that. Could I see some identification, please?

c1
R Good evening, sir. How can I help you?
G I have a reservation in my name. Scott. George Scott.
R Mr Scott. Let me see … Yes, here you are. A twin-bedded room, non-smoking, three nights.
G That's right.
R Could I just see some identification, please, Mr Scott …

c2
R Good evening, sir. How can I help you?
G I have a reservation in my name. Scott. George Scott.
R Mr Scott. Let me see … Yes, here you are. A twin-bedded room, non-smoking, three nights.
G That's right.
R Could I just see some identification, please, Mr Scott?
G Here you are.
R OK. And will you be using the garage?
G No.
R Will you be paying by credit card?
G Yes. American Express.
R Could I just have your card a moment, please, to swipe it?
G Yes, of course. Here you are.
R OK. And if you could just sign here on the registration card? Good. And this is your key card. Remember not to keep them together for security. Ehm, breakfast is from six-thirty to nine-thirty. The breakfast room is in the basement. Er, the restaurant is here on the ground floor. The lifts are over there next to the concierge's desk. Welcome to the Monumental.
G Thank you.
R Not at all. Have a nice stay.

Unit 2 Pronunciation

1 Good evening, sir. How can I help you?
2 Could I just see some identification, please, Mr Scott?
3 And will you be using the garage?
4 Will you be paying by credit card?
5 Could I just have your card a moment, please, to swipe it?

6 And if you could just sign here on the registration card?

7 And this is your key card.

Unit 2 Language spot

Where things are

G = Guest, R = Receptionist

1

G Could you tell me where the hairdresser's is?

R Certainly, madam. It's in the basement between the newsagent's and Meeting room 1.

G Thank you.

R You're welcome.

2

G Excuse me. Is there a gift shop here?

R Yes, sir. It's in the basement opposite the hairdresser's.

3

G Excuse me. Where's Meeting room 1?

R In the basement at the end of the corridor, madam.

Unit 2 Listening

The staff structure of hotels

I = Interviewer, R = Roberta

I Roberta, can you tell us a little about the staffing at the Concordia?

R Well, the Hotel Concordia's part of a larger group so we've got the same structure as the other hotels in the chain. It's a medium-sized hotel, and it's divided into three departments – front office, housekeeping, and food and beverages. Food and beverages covers the restaurant, bar, cafeteria, and the kitchen. In the kitchen we've got a head chef, Giovanni, and three junior chefs. There are two kitchen assistants, as well. Then for the restaurant and bars, we have a head waiter and six waiters.

I What about housekeeping?

R That's divided into maintenance and rooms. At the moment, there's one person in maintenance, Enrico, and on rooms there's the head housekeeper, Carlotta, and her team. She's got five housekeepers working for her right now, though in the high season we usually contract two more.

I You use the term *housekeeper*. Is that the same as *chambermaid*?

R Yes, and in the past housekeepers were usually called chambermaids. But we

prefer *housekeeper*. We're talking about trained professionals here, and the idea of a *maid* sounds more like a servant than a paid professional.

I What about the reception? Or should I say front office?

R For the ordinary client, it's the reception, obviously. But for us in the hotel trade, it's the *front office*. Now, here at the Hotel Concordia, the front office is run by Luigi, the Front Office Manager. He's got six receptionists working under him, and Silvio, the concierge.

I The concierge? What does he do?

R As well as carrying bags to guests' rooms, a concierge runs information services for the guests, or he gets them tickets for shows, for the theatre, he takes messages … things like that.

I And Silvio does all this?

R Yes, he does. And he does it very well. Better still, if we are very busy, he also acts as an extra receptionist.

I Roberta, thanks for your time.

R Not at all.

Unit 3 Listening

Tourist information

1

A Good morning. You're through to the rail information line. This is Wayne speaking. How can I help you?

B Hello, I'd like to find out about availability for a trip to Manchester tomorrow.

A Certainly, madam. What time will you be travelling?

B Around nine in the morning.

A Fine, how many in the party?

B Two adults and one child.

A OK, I'll just check for you …

2

A Of course, madam. The maps are down there to your left, on the shelf next to the guidebooks.

B Oh, yes. Thank you.

A You're welcome. Is there anything else I can help you with?

B No, that's all, thank you.

3

A Do you need any help?

B We were just looking for some information on places to eat in the evening, where we can take the kids.

A I see. How old are they?

B Two and four.

A Have a look through this guidebook. They've got a list of places with different facilities, including high chairs and so on.

B Mm. Thanks.

A If you need any more information, I'll be over at the desk.

4

… for information on our Book-a-bed-ahead service, please press 4 to speak to an assistant.

A Hello. My name's Susan. Can I have your name, please?

B Koller, Kristina Koller.

A Hello, Kristina. What destination are you looking for?

B Edinburgh.

A OK. What night?

B Next Tuesday.

A That's the 15th. And how many nights?

B Just one – a single room.

A OK, and do you have a price range in mind?

B Nothing too expensive, but I would like en suite.

A OK, Kristina. We have several options coming up …

5

Welcome to the Tate Gallery information line. For information about Tate Britain, press 1. For information about Tate Modern, press 2. For information about Tate Liverpool, press 3. For information about Tate St Ives, press 4. To book tickets for special exhibitions, press zero to be transferred to an assistant. Up-to-date information is available on our website at www.tate.org.uk.

Unit 3 Listening

How do I get to … ?

a

When you come out of the Information Centre, turn right and go down the High Street. Walk on through the Market Place until you come to a fork in the road. If you take the right-hand fork and go along Queen Street, you'll go past some nice antique shops and a small art gallery and eventually you'll come to a green hill. Head up the hill past the cannon and you're there. There are some lovely views along the coastline.

b

The best way is to cut through Church Street – it's just over there to the right; can you see it? If you turn right at the end of Church Street, you'll go past a lovely little green and you'll see the lighthouse – you can't miss it. Just walk towards the lighthouse and then the seafront is just ahead of you. When you get to the seafront, turn left, and you can either walk along the beach or the cliff. You'll see it in the distance sticking out to sea. It shouldn't take you any longer than fifteen minutes.

Unit 3 Pronunciation

1 come out of
2 walk on
3 head up
4 turn right out of
5 turn left at

Unit 4 Listening

A rep for all seasons

Exercise 2

1
Hi. I'm Jason. My job means that I have to look after people of all ages. Obviously I look after families, but I also take care of small groups of men or women on holiday. You have to be a people person to do this type of work.

2
My name's Luke McClure, and my job is to make sure that groups of men and women aged between 18 and 35 have the time of their life on holiday. There are loads of different names for what I do – it depends on the tour company. Right now I'm a Club 18–30 rep.

3
Hi. I'm Katerina Mattheoudakis. I'm the person that takes holidaymakers to and from the airport. Actually, it's a very important job because normally I'm the first person they see. I represent the tour operator so I've always got to be friendly and approachable. During the coach trips to the resorts …

4
I'm Anne Marie. What I do is very similar to being a family rep, except that we are always outside, even in the rain. Apart from the usual reps' duties, I'm responsible for montage – that's French for putting up tents – and de-montage – French for – surprise! – taking them down again.

Exercise 3

Jason
The main duties of a family rep? Well, obviously the first thing is transfers to and from the airport. And on the first morning I run a Welcome meeting where I tell people about the hotel and the area. I also try to sell excursions then, because I get commission on them if I do. I guide excursions – not all of the ones I sell, but two or three each week. Let's see … I check the accommodation and do any safety checks, as well. And I have to be ready 24/7 to answer the customers' queries and solve their problems.

Luke
As a club rep my main responsibilities are answering customers' queries and doing the Welcome meeting. That's a great chance for reps to sell events and things like T-shirts, hats, sunglasses. I suppose the thing I like most is organizing entertainment. We do pool parties, themed party nights, we take customers to discos – and we make sure they all come home! There's bar crawls … Of course, I do transfers. Not much fun. And then there's what I like least, which is cabaret. I don't mind the singing. But some of the games … Well, it wouldn't be my choice.

Unit 4 Listening

Welcome to paradise!

OK, everybody. There's one thing left on this morning's agenda – the welcome meeting, which the resort's reps do in pairs. Now I know that this isn't so important for you people as transfer reps because this year you won't be doing this. But you will be helping the resort reps from time to time, so please do listen.

OK, so let's imagine we've just dropped off the last of the new arrivals. So, go back to the main hotel and find the resort manager – for those of you going out to Crete, that's me of course. Hi! It's really important to do this as there may have been last-minute changes in the meeting arrangements.

After finding the resort manager, go to the meeting room and make sure the complimentary drinks are ready. Also check you have the right paperwork with you. You'd be surprised how easy it is to start a meeting and then realize you've got the wrong notes.

As people start arriving, greet them with a friendly smile and welcome them to the meeting. This should last around 25 minutes – certainly no longer – and should be informative and interesting. Your personality has to come through strongly here. Remember, they'll be tired, so if you're not good, they'll lose interest quickly.

Start by talking about the hotels. Next, talk a bit about the resort and the area, the places to go, and so on. Once you've got them interested in getting out of the swimming pool, tell them about the excursions. Encourage people to book as many excursions as possible because this is where you earn commission. We'll be looking at sales techniques tomorrow morning.

OK, bring the meeting to a close, take any spontaneous bookings for excursions, and then stay for a while to see if anybody has any questions. Relax now, and socialize briefly. The more people get to know you, the better you can do your job. The better you do your job, the happier I am.

Unit 4 Pronunciation

1 arrangements
2 arrivals
3 changes
4 customers
5 drinks
6 excursions
7 facilities
8 notes
9 places

Unit 5 Listening

Our national dish

1
I think it's great to see Japanese restaurants opening all over the world. I really love our food, especially sushi, which is our national dish. And I also really like sashimi – which is just raw fish. That's fantastic, too.

2
The problem with curry is that it isn't really Indian. At least, what a lot of non-Indians understand by the word *curry* isn't really much like what we eat in our homes in India. And to a lot of people, the word *curry* means something hot and spicy, but a lot of Indian dishes are very mild, and use yogurt or cream.

3
There are so many dishes here that it's hard to say what our national dish is. But the basic food of ordinary Mexicans is tortillas. We eat them with a meal like bread. They're used in lots of typical dishes – baked for enchiladas, fried for tacos, or grilled for quesadillas.

Unit 5 Pronunciation

Exercise 1
sea   sort   spot

Exercise 2
1 cheese
2 courgette
3 course
4 cream
5 lobster
6 meat
7 olive
8 oranges
9 pork
10 prawns

Unit 5 Listening

Describing dishes

1
A Are you ready to order?
B Almost, but can you tell me what a Wiener schnitzel is?
A Wiener schnitzel. It's meat. It's a kind of beef – a slice of young beef … I think you say 'veal'.
B Oh, it's veal!
A Yes, veal. The meat is covered in breadcrumbs and then fried in butter. Sometimes the breadcrumbs are seasoned with black pepper.
B Does it come with anything? Any vegetables?
A Yes. Schnitzel is served with potato salad and a slice of lemon. If you want, you can also have roast potatoes, French fries, or rice.
B Hmm. Sounds nice. And what is …

2
A Hello again. Have you had a chance to look at the menu?
B Yes, but there are things we don't understand.
A That's no problem. I'll try to explain them.
B OK, can you tell us what tagines are?
A Yes, that's meat – normally it's chicken or beef – and it's cooked with potatoes, carrots, and perhaps some other vegetables. It's a type of stew. Tagines are the pots that it's cooked in.
B Mm, that sounds OK. And harira?
A Harira is a bit like tomato soup, but it's got other vegetables in it, too.
B Mm, that would be nice as a starter. And the salade Marocaine?
A A salade Marocaine is normally made of chopped tomatoes, onions, green peppers, and cucumber. But here we also add boiled potatoes and olives. It's very nice.
B OK. Can we have another five minutes while we choose?
A Yes, of course. There's no hurry.

Unit 5 Listening

How to deal with complaints

H = Head waiter, **A, B, C, D** = trainee waiters
H OK, everybody. Let's talk about complaints and how we're going to deal with them. Of course, most important of all is to accept them. Complaints are a way of getting better, so be positive. Secondly, most complaints are about things that are easy to do something about. And for the really difficult complaints, you've got me. So, put

yourselves in the situation. You've got a customer complaining. What's the first step?
A Let the customer speak.
H Good. That's right. Listen, without interrupting. And show the customer that you're listening. What's next?
A Apologize.
H Good. Apologize. For example?
B Say *I'm sorry* or *I'm very sorry*.
H And apologize with care in your voice. Feel it. Feel sorry. Now, the third stage. What about questions?
C We only ask relevant questions, and we shouldn't ask too many questions.
H Well, you have been doing your homework. Great. But there is one essential time to ask questions.
D If we're not clear about what the customer wants us to do, we ask questions to make sure we understand completely.
H Well done. Now, the last thing. What about giving the customer a solution to the problem? Let's see … let's say the cutlery is dirty.
B We say something like *I'm very sorry. I'll change it right away.*
H Or they asked for water and you forgot about it?
C *I'm very sorry. I'll get it right away. I do apologize.*
H Excellent. I can see we're going to have a great summer together.

Unit 6 Listening

Local people and rural tourism

1
I love my job because I can work here in my village. We used to come and play around this church when I was a little girl, but I never thought that I would one day be the guide. I studied in Heraklion and got my diploma in tourism. And then the town council decided they needed a guide because the church is important, even though it is small. So now I'm living and working in the village I was born in. I love that.

2
Rural tourism is a good opportunity for this part of Thailand. Visitors to Umphang can see the way of life of the local hill people. These people – the Karen hill tribe – keep elephants as a means of transportation and they live very close to nature. And there are other activities for rural tourism like trekking, rafting, and nature-watching. All these activities help to make this a potential area for ecotourism.

3
Rural tourism has given new life to an old industry here in Tamil Nadu. In the past in this part of India, people made many things from the banana tree.

A lot of our traditional foods are made from banana. And we make baskets from fibre that we make from the banana tree leaves. My mother and grandmother made baskets, and now I am learning to do it too.

Unit 6 Listening

Checking in at a campsite

1
R = Receptionist, **M** = Mrs Crowshaw
R Hello. Can I help you?
M Yes, we booked a place online. The name's Crowshaw.
R Crowshaw. Let me just get your file … Here you are. Two adults, two children, two weeks. And it's one pitch for a motorhome, and a second pitch for a family tent.
M Two pitches, that's right. But it's not a family tent. It's a small tent – for the children.
R Oh. I'll just change it. There you are. One motorhome, and one small tent. Now could you give me your passport for a moment?
M Of course. Here you are.
R Will you be using an electric hook-up?
M Yes.
R Do you want that on both pitches?
M No, only on the motorhome pitch.
R OK. Could you just sign here, please? OK. This is for you. It's your registration card. Can you hang it over the door of the tent, please? You're in Zone B in pitches thirty-four and thirty-five …

2
T = Tourist, **R** = Receptionist
T Hello. Are you full?
R We've got some space until Friday. What were you looking for?
T There are four of us. We've got tents.
R Are they family tents?
T No, no. They're small tents. They're mountain tents.
R And is that four tents?
T No. Only two.
R OK. So that's two small tents until Friday. That's four nights. I'll put you all on one pitch to save you money.
T Oh, good.
R Have you got a car?
T No, we've got bikes.
R Motorbikes?
T No, they're normal bikes. You know, pedal bikes.

R Goodness! Isn't it a bit hot for cycling?
T Not in the morning.
R But in the afternoon…?
T In the afternoon, we go to the swimming pool. Do you have a swimming pool?
R Yes, of course. We've got …

Unit 6 Pronunciation

Exercise 1
R Here you are. Two adults, two children, two weeks. And it's one pitch for a motorhome, and a second pitch for a family tent.
M Two pitches, that's right. But it's not a family tent. It's a small tent – for the children.
R Oh. I'll just change it. There you are. One motorhome, and one small tent.

Exercise 3
T There are four of us. We've got tents.
R Are they family tents?
T No, no. They're small tents. They're mountain tents.
R And is that four tents?
T No. Only two.
R Have you got a car?
T No, we've got bikes.
R Motorbikes?
T No, they're normal bikes. You know, pedal bikes.

Unit 6 Listening

Forecasting the weather
A Excuse me, but do you know what the weather will be like tomorrow?
B Well, I think it'll be like today … Clear and bright in the morning, lots of sunshine, and then getting cloudy again in the afternoon. But I think we'll see a few thundery storms tomorrow afternoon. It's very humid at the moment.
A Thundery?
B You know … Bang and crash. Clouds making a noise.
A Oh, *Donnerschlag*. Will it stay like that all week?
B No, I don't think so. They said it's going to rain on Thursday. And it's going to get a bit colder so that will stop the storms.
A Oh. Rain.
B Don't worry. There's lots to do here even when it rains. Have you been to the mine museum or …?

Unit 7 Pronunciation

1	coast	6	Shakespeare
2	home	7	Shakespeare
3	lake	8	stadium
4	parade	9	stately
5	Rome	10	theatre

Unit 7 Listening

Describing a festival

Good morning, everyone. Welcome to Venice. My name is Carlotta and I'll be your guide for this weekend when we see the Festa del Redentore, the Festival of the Redeemer, the high point of the Venice summer, with its spectacular firework display.

Before I start: can you all hear me at the back? Good. OK, let me start by telling you a little about the history of the festival.

From 1575 to 77, as you may know, Venice was hit by a devastating plague. It killed more than a third of the city's inhabitants. In 1576, the city's leader, the Doge, promised to build a church dedicated to the Redeemer, in return for help in ending the plague. On July 13th, 1577, the plague was declared over, and work began to build the church. It was also decided that Venice would forever give thanks on the third Sunday of July.

Now, moving on to the festival itself. What happens is this: from early on the Saturday, boats are decorated with flowers, lanterns, and balloons. St Mark's lagoon fills with as many as two thousand boats. You'll see their occupants eating and drinking as they wait for the traditional spectacular display of fireworks. By the way, if you're wondering about dinner on Saturday evening, you can make arrangements with the hotel for dinner on a boat. At around 11.30 p.m., the display begins. You'll see fireworks illuminating the silhouetted spires, domes, and bell towers of the city.

On Sunday, you'll see a pontoon of decorated gondolas and other boats strung across the Giudecca canal. This is to allow the faithful to walk to the church of the Redentore. The climax of the festival, and the most significant part if you remember what I said about the history of the festival, is the mass held in the presence of the Patriarch of Venice. This is a reminder that the Festa has a serious side.

Oh, one thing I forgot to mention is that the traditional food for Saturday night is roast duck, watermelon, and of course wine. So, that's the Festa del Redentore. As you can see, it's a wonderful event. OK, are there any questions?

Unit 8 Listening

From tour guide to tour manager

I've always been interested in tourism, so when I left school, I took a Coach Tour Guide Course at college. This is a pretty thorough course and, in fact, people come from all over Europe to study on it because the qualification you get is accepted in many other European countries.

Competition for the vacancies is tough – I didn't get the job I wanted right away. Then I saw an ad for a company offering 18 to 35 coach tours of Europe, and applied. I didn't actually need my qualification to apply, but you had to have experience of travelling in Europe. I'd been around France, Germany, Italy, and the Czech Republic in the holidays and I think this went in my favour.

My first year was as Tour Guide, working under a Tour Manager. This year I'm a Tour Manager, which means I'm in charge of a Tour Guide, a driver, and a coach of up to 50 holidaymakers on a fourteen-day tour of Europe.

We do everything, including providing a commentary, organizing excursions and parties, and checking everybody in and out of the pre-booked accommodation along the way. It's great fun, but it's most definitely hard work – it's never a holiday for us!

Unit 8 Listening

Practicalities on tour

a
S = Sarah, R = Receptionist
S Hi, this is Sarah, the guide from Galloway Tours. I'm just checking you got my message about the later arrival tonight.
R Let me see … yes, you're not getting in until 9.00 p.m. – is that correct?
S Yes, and did you get the message about the late dinner as well?
R Yes, we've booked you a supper for 9.30 in the bar.
S Great. While I've got you, can I just check something else? There's some confusion on the rooming list. Erm, in the printout I've got Mr and Mrs Sandford in separate rooms, but it should be a double.
R Did you say Mr and Mrs Sandford?
S Yeah.
R OK … No, we've got them for a double.
S Oh good, and will that have a double bed or twins?

R A double bed.
S Thank you very much.
R You're welcome.

b
Welcome, everybody. Can you all hear me OK? Yes? Good. Let me start by introducing myself – my name's Sarah and I'll be looking after you today. Your driver today is Ken. We're going to be on the coach quite a lot today because we're taking a scenic route through the countryside, so I hope you're all comfortable. Is the temperature OK? Good. We will be stopping for lunch in a very nice hilltop restaurant, and after a visit to the castle in the afternoon, we should arrive at tonight's hotel around 6.00 p.m.
I'll be telling you a little bit about the countryside and some of the places we pass, but for the moment, just sit back and relax. Once we're under way, I'll be passing through the coach, so if you have any questions about the day, please ask me.

c
If you look to your left in a moment, you'll see the top of Ben Nevis, which is the highest mountain in the British Isles, at a height of 1,344 metres. It's cold at the top! Now, one of the ladies was asking me about the Scottish kilt, so I'll tell you something about this traditional dress, which is of course still worn by many men today …

d
Hi, this is Sarah again. There's another problem. The first driver's over his hours, so we're going to have to take a two-hour break until the relief driver can get here. Is that OK? It's a nice place with some good shops, so I don't think the passengers mind. I'm assuming it'll be all right to get them each a complimentary drink. If that's a problem, call me back on the mobile. Thanks.

e
OK, thank you for listening. I hope you've enjoyed the first part of the tour. We're going to take a break here. You'll find a café and toilets in the buildings over to the left of the coach. Please be back on the coach in thirty minutes' time – that's at, er, eleven o'clock. Did you all get that? Eleven o'clock. The coach departs at 11.05 precisely in order to meet our train connection. There'll be a lot of coaches parked here, so make sure you know which one is ours – we're displaying the number 64, OK? Now, please be careful as you get off, the steps are rather steep, and the road outside is a bit slippery. Thank you.

Unit 8 Listening

Problems on tour

G = Guide, P = Mrs Parsons

G OK, ladies and gentlemen. I'm very sorry about this, but as you can see we have a bit of a problem. Let me explain the situation. Unfortunately the coach has broken down and we're going to have to wait for a relief coach. Now, please keep calm. There's nothing to worry about as the company assure me the relief coach will be here in less than an hour. I know it's very hot on the coach. So this is what we're going to do: we're going to leave the coach and go up the bank to rest in the shade of the trees up on your left. But we have to be very careful as we're on a busy motorway. Um, the driver will lead you up the bank. I hope that's clear? So starting from the front … oh, yes, and leave your bags on the coach, just take your valuables and any water if you have any … Oh dear, what's the matter?
P I'm not sure I can climb up that bank. I've got a bad leg.
G OK, please don't worry, Mrs Parsons. Just sit here for a while. We'll let the others off first.
P But I really don't think I can get up there.
G I know, I understand. Um, I'll tell you what we'll do. When everyone else is off you can stay on the coach and sit at the front – with the door open, you'll be cool. Would you prefer that?
P Oh, yes dear, that would be lovely.
G OK. Now just wait here and try to relax. Here are some tissues. I'll get some water for you.
P Thank you so much.

Unit 8 Pronunciation

Exercise 1
1 a I'm sorry about this.
  b I'm really sorry about this.
2 a There's nothing to worry about.
  b There's really nothing to worry about.
3 a That sounds terrible.
  b That sounds really terrible.
4 a I do apologize.
  b I really do apologize.

Exercise 2
1 a I'm really sorry about this.
  b I'm really sorry about this.
2 a There's really nothing to worry about.
  b There's really nothing to worry about.

3 a That sounds really terrible.
  b That sounds really terrible.
4 a I really do apologize.
  b I really do apologize.

Unit 9 Pronunciation

Exercise 1
scuba diving   sports
skating   swimming

Exercise 2
kids   practised
adult   went

Unit 9 Listening

Making a water ball

OK. Are you all listening? Have you all got your balloons? Has everybody got a pair of scissors? Yes? So, blow up one of the balloons to stretch it a little. Give it a good stretch. That's it. Good. Now, once you've stretched the balloon, fill it with water and tie a knot. When you tie the knot, try to make the shape of the balloon as round as possible. Do you see what I mean? Look at mine. Can I help you, Pedro? OK, that's good. Now get the scissors and cut the tail of the balloon. That's right. Cut the tail. Good.

Now get another balloon, blow it up, let the air out, and when you've let the air out, place the first balloon inside it. Work in twos and help each other. One of you hold the second balloon as open as possible, and the other one put the first balloon inside. That's it. Lovely. OK. So, now, cut the tail of the second balloon. No, there's no need to tie it this time. Have you all done that? Yes? OK. So now do this again and again until you've used up all the balloons. Who needs help? Marianne, Pierre – you OK?

When you've finished, what you've got is a ball that bounces and that's really good for practising juggling. If you drop it, it bounces back and you don't have to bend over to pick it up.

Unit 9 Listening

Getting the job

Q = Interviewer, I = Ineke

Q Ineke, what attracted you to the job of entertainment worker?

I Well, I wanted to practise what I'd been studying at university, especially my foreign languages. And I wanted to earn a bit of money.

Q And what was it like in Bali?

I It was a fantastic experience. At first I was a bit nervous because it was the first time I was going to be so far away from home for such a long time … But everything worked out fine.

Q How did you find the job?

I I put my CV on a web page for jobs in tourism, and an agency in Holland emailed me with the job in Bali.

Q There was an initial selection process. What was that like?

I Well, we had a personal interview in Rotterdam and a series of tests – how you did with a microphone, what sort of initiative you had, what sort of person you were …. And then after the interview they asked me to go to the training sessions.

Q There was specific training for the job?

I Yes. They showed us everything we were going to do … how to organize games, how to keep groups under control, how to use a microphone.

Q Really?

I Yes, how to hold the microphone, the tone of voice you use, how you had to stand on stage … because most of us were beginners. We'd never held a microphone.

Q So the training was good.

I It was tough, but it was excellent.

Q And did you like the job?

I I loved it. The atmosphere, the way my colleagues were always there to help, the hotel … I loved it. And they had everything organized. It was hard to come home, in fact.

Unit 10 Listening

Special requests

1 A I need a new battery for my camera. Can we stop at a shop before we get to the shoot?

B That shouldn't be a problem. I'll just check with the driver.

2 A Can we take some of these plants back with us?

B Sorry, you can't. They're a protected species: you mustn't remove them from their natural habitat.

3 A I said no to the trip down the diamond mine, but I've changed my mind. Can I join it?

B Of course. No problem. I'll add your name to the list straightaway.

4 A Would it be OK to take some pictures inside the cathedral?

B I don't see why not. There might be a problem if there's a service on – and you may need to pay something. I'll ask when we go in.

5 A I've noticed there's an extra wine-tasting course next weekend. Is there any chance of me extending my holiday and staying on for it?

B I'm not sure. We may possibly be able to make arrangements. I'll have to check with my head office.

Unit 10 Pronunciation

Exercise 2

1	car park	7	hearing aid
2	guide dog	8	light switch
3	doorway	9	sign language
4	footpath	10	walkway
5	hand-rail	11	welcome talk
6	health spa	12	wheelchair

Exercise 3

1 specially adapted
2 purpose-built
3 hearing impaired
4 remote control

Unit 10 Listening

Disability access

M = Michael, J = Jane

M Hatton Hall Hotel, Michael speaking. How can I help you?

J Hi, this is Jane Wicks. I'm the guide bringing the Access for All adventure group at the weekend. I'm just calling to check a few things.

M Oh, yes. I think everything's set up for them.

J That's good. I just need to run through a few things. We've got three wheelchair users, but all the group – that's ten in all – have mobility difficulties of some sort, so we need to be accommodated in ground-floor rooms. Is that going to be OK?

M Yes, no problem. All the ground-floor rooms have recently been adapted to allow for wheelchair use. They've got wide doors, automatic opening, and low-level switches.

J Great. Are the other facilities all OK for the group?

M Yes, mostly. Toilets and all the signage conform to regulations. The bar on the top floor still needs upgrading, because the lift doesn't go that far. But there's a bar on the ground floor and the restaurant has been renovated, and we've got ramps and hand-rails in all public areas – except the garden

that is: that still needs to be upgraded. Oh, and another thing, we're making some changes to the reception area at the moment, so I'm afraid the low-level reception desk is out of action. Is that going to be a problem?

J No, I don't think so. I'll be doing a group check-in. But the group will need to come through reception – is that OK?

M It's only the desk that's affected. The whole entrance area has been adapted – ramps and so on – so there's no need to worry.

J Good, I think that's it. Now I've got to call ahead to the activity centre to check things there. Thanks for your help.

M Pleasure. See you at the weekend.

Unit 11 Listening

The needs of the business traveller

I = Interviewer, C = Carlos Lozano

I What do business travellers look for most in a travel company?

C Mainly it's speed and efficiency, no fuss, not to have to worry about the arrangements. They want to be able to say 'we want this', and we do it. Ordinary tourists, maybe they want to spend time talking about the different possibilities – it's part of the fun for them, but not business travellers. They want to be able to book last minute, and 24 hours a day – and to make changes at the last minute – and things like express check-in and use of a business lounge at airports. They also want the personal touch. We allocate an account manager to each of our clients and they have all the client history at their fingertips, things like preferences on window or aisle seats, type of hotel room, meal options. We like to know our clients.

I Yes, that must be important.

C Yes, and it means we can arrange everything for them – flights, transfers, hotel, car hire, meeting rooms.

I So it's a kind of package.

C Not really a package, more of a menu – 'this is what we can offer – which services do you want us to arrange for you?'

I As far as hotel requirements go, what do business travellers tend to look for?

C Assuming the basics of comfort, cleanliness, fast internet access, and so on, the number one is location – centre of town, near to the airport, both of those if possible.

I Business travel has an image of luxury high costs, high expense accounts, and so on. Is that true?

C Certainly not. Businesses these days are looking for value for money. Of course, compared to regular tourists, they still tend to use higher quality accommodation and upgraded travel, particularly when entertaining important clients. For us it's a bit of balancing act – providing excellent quality and service, but not charging too much. But we find ways to go the extra mile.

I 'Go the extra mile'? What do you mean by that?

C Giving a little bit extra that will make them appreciate us and justify why they should use us rather than book direct over the Internet. For example, I've already mentioned the personal touch, but we also offer support services such as info packs on the place they're going to – simple fact sheets with practicalities of time difference, climate, transport services, visa and health requirements, and so on. Also, we produce a mini 'Culture Guide', covering basics of social etiquette and doing business with different cultures. It's proved very popular.

I That's very interesting. Thanks for talking to us, Carlos.

C You're welcome.

Unit 11 Pronunciation

1 pear	4 beach
2 bear	5 Ben
3 peach	6 pen

Unit 12 Listening

Life in the front office

I = Interviewer, E = Erika

I Erika, is there a lot of routine to front office work?

E There is if that's how you see it. Of course, all jobs have routines, and a receptionist is no different. But if we spent all day dealing with emergencies, we wouldn't last very long.

I And what are your routines?

E Checking guests in and out are the obvious ones. Then there's allocating parking spaces, controlling access to the garage, taking bookings …

I Taking messages?

E That used to be a routine, but nowadays everybody has mobile phones, so we don't get many messages.

I What about questions? Do you get many questions?

E More than you'd think. Of course, we get asked some questions again and again.

What can we see in the city? Can you recommend a restaurant? But answering questions is another chance to get to know your guests. In fact, when you monitor customer satisfaction, you often see comments that indicate that by making routine duties seem special, we make our guests feel important.

I Are you responsible for monitoring guest satisfaction?

E Not directly, but each day while they're checking out, we get four or five guests to complete a short questionnaire. And when guests have a problem, they come to reception first, so we get first-hand information about how the hotel is working.

I I suppose that dealing with problems is the worst of your duties?

E Yes and no. Dealing with problems is yet another chance to get to know your guests. But if we don't deal with them well, that can lead to a complaint, which is a totally different thing.

Unit 12 Listening

Common problems

R = Receptionist, G = Guest

Situation 1

R Reception. Can I help you?

G Hi, this is Room 418. I've just got into the room and, well, I asked for a non-smoking room.

R Just one minute, please. You are in 418?

G That's right.

R 418 is a non-smoking room, madam.

G Well, I'm afraid that somebody's been smoking in here. It smells really strongly of tobacco.

R Oh, I'm very sorry about that. Would you like to change rooms?

G Yes, I think I'd prefer that.

R OK. I'll issue a new key right away and get the porter to help you to change.

G Thanks very much.

R Not at all, madam. And I apologize for the inconvenience.

Situation 2

G Hi. It's cold in my room and I can't get the heating to come on.

R I'm afraid there's nothing I can do about it. The heating's off in the whole building until October.

G Until October! You're not serious? The weather forecast on TV said it would drop to 6 degrees tonight.

R I'll get the housekeeper to give you an extra blanket.

G Well, I'm grateful, but I don't want to get into bed yet. I need to work. You know, sitting at the table.

R Well, I'm sorry, but the only thing I can do is get you a blanket.

Unit 12 Pronunciation

a Could you put me through to room service, please?

b Have you any idea where I can get a good meal?

c Can you tell me the quickest way to the city centre?

d Do you think I could speak to the housekeeper?

e So I was wondering what you can do about it.

f Do you think you could get someone to come and look at it?

Unit 12 Listening

Can I have my bill?

G = Guest, R = Receptionist

G Hi there. Could I get my bill there? Room 705.

R 705? It's Mr Wiley, isn't it?

G Sure is.

R Did you have anything from the minibar last night?

G Nope.

R OK, Mr Wiley, I'm just printing your bill out. Has everything been to your satisfaction?

G Sure has.

R Oh, I'm glad. Will you be paying by credit card, Mr Wiley?

G Sure will.

R Could I just have your card for a moment?

G Yep. Here you are.

R OK. Here's your bill. Can I just ask you to check it?

G OK. Mm. Looks fine to me.

R So, if I could just ask you to sign here.

G There you go.

R Thank you. Here's your credit card and this is your copy of the payment slip. It's been a pleasure having you here.

G Thank you.

Glossary

Vowels

iː	seafront	ʊ	campsite courier	aɪ	sign
i	commentary	uː	bruised	aʊ	voucher
ɪ	disabled	u	gratuities	ɔɪ	olive oil
e	credit	ʌ	couple	ɪə	theatre-style
æ	rash	ɜː	sunburn	eə	visual impairment
ɑː	woodcarving	ə	item	ʊə	Tour Manager
ɒ	sausage	eɪ	baked		
ɔː	sore	əʊ	anecdote		

Consonants

p	pitch	f	feedback	h	hub
b	badge	v	variable	m	marble
t	tip	θ	thunder	n	niche
d	dish	ð	deal with	ŋ	dazzling
k	clipboard	s	seasonal	l	listings
g	garlic	z	hazard	r	ramp
tʃ	charge	ʃ	shower	j	yoghurt
dʒ	register	ʒ	audio-visual	w	welcome

access /ˈækses/ *n* a way of entering or reaching a place

account /əˈkaʊnt/ *n* 1. an arrangement with a business to pay for their products or services at a later time, for example at the end of each month 2. a record of the money owed to or paid to a company during a particular period

activity sheet /ækˈtɪvəti ʃiːt/ *n* a piece of paper with questions that you answer by doing particular tasks

adult /ˈædʌlt/ *n* a person who is eighteen years old or older

agency /ˈeɪdʒənsi/ *n* a company or an organization that arranges something on behalf of somebody else, for example a travel agency

allergic /əˈlɜːdʒɪk/ *adj* having a medical condition that causes you to react badly or feel sick when you eat or touch a particular substance

allocate /ˈæləkeɪt/ *v* to officially give something to somebody for a particular purpose, for example a room at a hotel or a seat at a table

anecdote /ˈænɪkdəʊt/ *n* a short, interesting, or amusing story about yourself or a real person / event

animatronics /ˌænɪməˈtrɒnɪks/ *n* the process of making and operating electronic models of people, animals, etc., used in films and other types of entertainment

aqua aerobics /ˌækwə eəˈrəʊbɪks/ *n* physical exercises done in water, usually in classes with music

arch /ɑːtʃ/ *n* 1. a curved structure with straight sides that supports something above it such as a bridge or the roof of a building 2. a curved structure with straight sides that is built as a **monument**

arrivals lounge /əˈraɪvlz ˌlaʊndʒ/ *n* a large room in an airport where people wait to meet passengers who are arriving or where passengers can sit and wait after they leave their plane

audio-tour /ˈɔːdiəʊ tʊə(r)/ *n* a small listening device which provides commentary while you walk around a museum, gallery, etc.

audio-visual /ˌɔːdiəʊ ˈvɪʒuəl/ *adj* using both sound and pictures

automatic (gears) /ɔːtəˌmætɪk ˈgɪəz/ *adj* (used about a car) having gears that operate without the need for direct action from the driver

badge /bædʒ/ *n* a small piece of metal or plastic, with a design or words on it, that a person wears and that may show their name, job title, etc.

baked /beɪkt/ *adj* cooked in an oven without extra fat or liquid

beef /biːf/ *n* meat that comes from a cow

bill /bɪl/ *n* a record that shows how much you owe for goods or services; a piece of paper on which this is written

blind /blaɪnd/ *adj* not able to see

boardroom /'bɔːdruːm/ *n* a room where the board of a company (= the people who control it) meet, usually round a long table

body language /'bɒdi ˌlæŋgwɪdʒ/ *n* the way you hold and move your body and what this communicates about your thoughts and feelings

border control /'bɔːdə kənˌtrəʊl/ *n* a place where officials check your passport, luggage, etc. when you cross from one country to another by road or on a train

Braille /breɪl/ *n* a system of printing for blind people that consists of raised marks on a page that are read by touch

break-out room /'breɪk aʊt ˌruːm/ *n* a place where a small group of people can meet that is separate from the main meeting room

bruised /bruːzd/ *adj* (used about a part of the body) having bruises (= purple marks that appear on the skin after you fall, are hit, etc.)

cabaret /'kæbəreɪ/ *n* entertainment with singing and dancing, performed in restaurants, cafes, and theatres

call centre /'kɔːl ˌsentə(r)/ *n* an office in which many people work using telephones, for example answering questions, taking customers' orders, etc.

campsite courier /ˌkæmpsaɪt 'kʊriə(r)/ *n* a person whose job is helping guests at a campsite (= a place where people on holiday stay in tents)

canyon /'kænjən/ *n* a deep valley with steep sides of rock

capacity /kə'pæsəti/ *n* the number of people that a room can hold

casino /kə'siːnəʊ/ *n* a building or room where people can play gambling games

CDW – collision damage waiver /siː diː 'dʌbljuː/ /kə'lɪʒn 'dæmɪdʒ 'weɪvə(r)/ *n* an insurance agreement in which the customer of a car rental company pays a sum of money so that if they have an accident, instead of paying the full cost of repairs, they only pay the **excess**

chalet host /'ʃæleɪ həʊst/ *n* a person whose job is taking care of guests at a chalet, a wooden guest house in a ski resort

chambermaid /'tʃeɪmbəmeɪd/ *n* an old-fashioned term for a **housekeeper** (1)

chance guest /'tʃɑːns gest/ *n* a guest who arrives at a hotel without a reservation for a room

charge /tʃɑːdʒ/ *v* to ask a specific amount of money for a product or service

charismatic /ˌkærɪz'mætɪk/ *adj* (used about a person) attractive and impressive to other people

check someone out /tʃek 'aʊt/ *v* to take back the room key, receive payment for a bill, etc., when a hotel guest is leaving for the last time

check-out process /'tʃek aʊt ˌprəʊses/ *n* the procedure of paying the bill, returning the room key, etc. when a guest leaves a hotel for the last time

child-friendly /tʃaɪld 'frendli/ *adj* (used about a place) safe and suitable for children

clarity /'klærəti/ *n* the quality of being clear and easily understood

cleanliness /'klenlinəs/ *n* the state of being clean

click (on) /klɪk/ *v* to choose a particular item on a computer screen by pressing one of the buttons on a mouse

clipboard /'klɪpbɔːd/ *n* a small board with a clip at the top for fastening papers, used so that you can write while standing

cloth /klɒθ/ *n* fabric / material made by **weaving** cotton, wool, silk, etc.

column /'kɒləm/ *n* 1. a tall post, usually made of stone, that supports the roof of a building or stands alone as a **monument** 2. one of the vertical sections into which a printed page, chart, etc. is divided

comfort break /'kʌmfət breɪk/ *n* a short period when a coach stops to allow passengers to go to the toilet, etc.

commentary /'kɒməntri/ *n* a spoken description of the buildings and places that you see when you go on a tour

complaint /kəm'pleɪnt/ *n* a statement in which somebody says that they are not satisfied with something

concierge /'kɒnsieəʒ/ *n* a person in a hotel whose job is to help guests by giving them information, arranging theatre tickets, etc.

configuration /kənˌfɪgə'reɪʃn/ *n* the way in which a group of things are arranged, for example a seating arrangement

conformity /kən'fɔːməti/ *n* agreement, for example by a client or customer that a bill is correct

construct /kən'strʌkt/ *v* to build or make something

corporate hospitality /ˌkɔːpərət hɒspɪ'tæləti/ *n* free entertainment given by a company to important clients, customers, etc. in order to establish or maintain a good relationship

cosmetic surgery /kɒzˌmetɪk 'sɜːdʒəri/ *n* medical treatment that involves cutting open part of the body (= surgery) to improve a person's appearance; the branch of medicine connected with this treatment

couple /'kʌpl/ *n* two people who have a romantic relationship with each other

course /kɔːs/ *n* one of the separate parts of a meal, such as a **starter** or a **dessert**

crafts worker /'krɑːfts ˌwɜːkə(r)/ *n* a person whose job involves a traditional skill of making things by hand, for example clothes or jewellery

credit /'kredɪt/ *n* money that has already been paid into an account

customer satisfaction /ˌkʌstəmə ˌsætɪsˈfækʃn/ *n* the extent to which a customer is pleased with a particular product or service

dazzling /'dæzlɪŋ/ *adj* very impressive and exciting

deaf /def/ *adj* not able to hear anything or not able to hear very well

deal with /'diːl wɪð/ *v* to take action to solve a problem

dedicated (to) /'dedɪkeɪtɪd tə/, /tu/ *adj* 1. working very hard for something because you think it is important 2. (used about a building such as a church) officially connected with a particular person as a sign of respect and admiration

delegate /'delɪɡət/ *n* a person who is attending a conference on behalf of an organization

depict /dɪ'pɪkt/ *v* to **represent** or describe something using words or pictures

designer /dɪ'zaɪnə(r)/ *adj* (used about clothes, jewellery, etc.) expensive, fashionable, and made by a famous designer

dessert /dɪ'zɜːt/ *n* sweet food eaten at the end of a meal, such as cake or ice cream

diabetic /ˌdaɪə'betɪk/ *adj* having diabetes (= a medical condition in which your body cannot process sugar properly)

diarrhoea /ˌdaɪə'rɪə/ *n* an illness in which you go to the toilet too often and empty solid waste matter from your body in liquid form

dimension /daɪ'menʃn/ *n* a measurement of space, for example the height, width, or length of a room

direct payment /dəˌrekt 'peɪmənt/ *n* the act of paying a hotel bill personally by cash, credit card, etc. rather than through an **agency**

disabled /dɪs'eɪbld/ *adj* 1. unable to use a part of your body completely or easily because of a physical condition, injury, etc. 2. (used about a place) designed to be used by disabled people

disco /'dɪskəʊ/ *n* a place where people can dance to recorded pop music

discriminate /dɪ'skrɪmɪneɪt/ *v* to unfairly treat one person better or worse than another, especially because of their race, sex, etc.

dish /dɪʃ/ *n* food cooked and prepared in a particular way as part of a meal

display rack /dɪ'spleɪ ræk/ *n* a piece of equipment, usually made of metal bars, that is used for holding and showing things

dizzy /'dɪzi/ *adj* feeling as if everything is spinning around you

dome /dəʊm/ *n* a curved roof with a circular base, for example on a church

door-to-door /'dɔː tə ˌdɔː/ *adj* involving transporting a person or thing directly from one place to another place

drop-off /'drɒp ɒf/ *n* the place where a person or thing is delivered or left

electric hook-up /ɪˌlektrɪk 'hʊk ʌp/ *n* an outside connection where you put a plug so that a machine can receive electricity, used, for example with **motorhomes**

entertainment /ˌentə'teɪnmənt/ *n* enjoyable or interesting activities

erect /ɪ'rekt/ *v* to build something such as a **monument**

excess /ɪk'ses/ *n* the part of an insurance claim that a customer must pay; SEE **CDW – collision damage waiver**

exhibition /ˌeksɪ'bɪʃn/ *n* an event at which a collection of things, such as different products, are shown to the public

exhilarating /ɪɡ'zɪləreɪtɪŋ/ *adj* extremely exciting and enjoyable

eye contact /'aɪ ˌkɒntækt/ *n* the act of looking into somebody's eyes at the same time as they look at you

façade /fə'sɑːd/ *n* the front of a building

FAQs /ˌef eɪ 'kjuːz/ *n* an abbreviation that stands for 'frequently asked questions'

feedback /'fiːdbæk/ *n* advice, criticism, and information from customers about what they thought of your product or service

first aid kit /ˌfɜːst 'eɪd ˌkɪt/ *n* a box containing medical materials such as bandages, kept in case somebody is injured

fitness centre /'fɪtnəs ˌsentə(r)/ *n* a place where people go to do physical exercise in order to stay fit and healthy

flavour /'fleɪvə(r)/ *n* how food or drink tastes

flip chart /'flɪp tʃɑːt/ *n* large sheets of paper fixed at the top to a stand so that you can turn them over, used for presenting information at a meeting

fog /fɒɡ/ *n* a thick cloud of very fine drops of water on the land or at sea, that is difficult to see through

food and beverages /ˌfuːd ən 'bevərɪdʒɪz/ *n* the department in a hotel that is responsible for providing food and drinks (= beverages) to guests, including the restaurant, bar, and kitchen

forecast /'fɔːkɑːst/ *n* a prediction of what the weather will be like

foreign exchange /ˌfɒrən ɪks'tʃeɪndʒ/ *n* the act of exchanging the money of one country for that of another country; the money of another country, exchanged in this way

forest /'fɒrɪst/ *n* a large area of land that is covered with trees

front office /frʌnt 'ɒfɪs/ *n* the department of a hotel that deals with the public, especially the reception desk

gala banquet /'ɡɑːlə ˌbæŋkwɪt/ *n* a formal meal for a large number of people to celebrate a special occasion

garlic /'ɡɑːlɪk/ *n* a white vegetable of the onion family, used in cooking to give **flavour** to food

genealogy /ˌdʒiːniˈælədʒi/ *n* the study of family history and of who a person's ancestors were

gesture /ˈdʒestʃə(r)/ *n* a movement that you make with your hands, your head, or your face that has a particular meaning

grading system /ˈɡreɪdɪŋ ˌsɪstəm/ *n* a method of placing hotels and restaurants into groups according to quality, service, etc.

grats (gratuities) /ɡræts/ /ɡrəˈtjuːətiːz/ *n* extra money given by a customer to an employee to thank them for the work that the employee has done; SEE **tip**

grilled /ɡrɪld/ *adj* cooked directly underneath a strong heat or on metal bars placed directly over a fire

guest history /ɡest ˈhɪstri/ *n* information about a guest's previous visits to a hotel

guest status /ɡest ˈsteɪtəs/ *n* the level of importance of a particular guest for a hotel

guide dog /ˈɡaɪd dɒɡ/ *n* a dog trained to help a **blind** person to walk around

guidelines /ˈɡaɪdlaɪnz/ *n* rules or instructions that tell you how to deal with certain situations

hand-rail /ˈhænd reɪl/ *n* a long narrow bar attached to a wall that you can hold on to for support

handshake /ˈhændʃeɪk/ *n* an act of shaking somebody's hand with your own, for example when saying hello or goodbye

hazard /ˈhæzəd/ *n* a possible risk or danger

health and safety checks /helθ ən ˈseɪfti tʃeks/ *n* regular actions that you must do by law to ensure that a place is safe for guests and employees

hearing aid /ˈhɪərɪŋ eɪd/ *n* a small device that fits inside the ear, used to help **deaf** people to hear better

hearing impairment /ˈhɪərɪŋ ɪmˌpeəmənt/ *n* a physical condition which prevents you from hearing normally

helpline /ˈhelp laɪn/ *n* a telephone service that you can call for advice about particular problems

home page /ˈhəʊm peɪdʒ/ *n* the main page on a website (= a place on the Internet where somebody puts information) with connections to other pages on the site

home stay /ˈhəʊm steɪ/ *n* the act of staying in a private house as a paying guest

hospitality /ˌhɒspɪˈtæləti/ *n* friendly and generous behaviour towards guests

housekeeper /ˈhaʊskiːpə(r)/ *n* 1. a person whose job is to clean bedrooms in a hotel 2. a person who manages the cooking, cleaning, etc. in a hotel

hub /hʌb/ *n* a central station or airport in a transport system where passengers can change planes, trains, etc. in order to travel to other places

identification /aɪˈdentɪfɪkeɪʃn/ *n* an official paper, document, etc. that is proof of who you are

initiative /ɪˈnɪʃətɪv/ *n* the ability to make decisions and act on your own without waiting for somebody to tell you what to do

interactive /ˌɪntərˈæktɪv/ *adj* allowing information to be passed in both directions between a computer and the person using it

item /ˈaɪtəm/ *n* a particular product or service that is listed on a bill

key card /ˈkiː kɑːd/ *n* a plastic card with a magnetic strip for opening a door

kid /kɪd/ *n* a child or a young person

kitchen assistant /ˈkɪtʃɪn əˌsɪstənt/ *n* a person whose job involves doing general work in a kitchen

lamb /læm/ *n* meat that comes from a young sheep

lamination /ˌlæmɪˈneɪʃn/ *n* the act of covering paper or card with a thin transparent layer of plastic for protection

laptop /ˈlæptɒp/ *n* a small computer that can be easily carried and used when travelling

leaflet /ˈliːflət/ *n* a free printed sheet of paper, usually folded, that advertises or gives information about something

learning difficulty /ˈlɜːnɪŋ ˌdɪfɪkəlti/ *n* a mental problem that affects somebody's ability to learn things

lighthouse /ˈlaɪthaʊs/ *n* a tall tower near the sea that shines a strong light in order to guide ships

listings /ˈlɪstɪŋz/ *n* an official published list of organizations, used for reference

low-level /ˌləʊ ˈlevl/ *adj* close to the ground

main course /ˌmeɪn ˈkɔːs/ *n* the most important **dish** of a meal

maintenance /ˈmeɪntənəns/ *n* the department in a hotel that is responsible for keeping the rooms and building in good condition by checking or repairing things

manual (gears) /ˈmænjuəl ˌɡɪəz/ *adj* (used about a car) operated or controlled by hand rather than automatically

marble /ˈmɑːbl/ *n* a type of hard stone, usually white with coloured lines in it, that can be polished and used for making **statues**, decorating buildings, etc.

maritime /ˈmærɪtaɪm/ *adj* connected with ships and sailing

meadow /ˈmedəʊ/ *n* a field covered in grass

microphone /ˈmaɪkrəfəʊn/ *n* a device used for making your voice louder when you are speaking to an audience

mobility /məʊˈbɪləti/ *n* the ability to move or travel around easily

monument /ˈmɒnjumənt/ *n* a public building, **statue**, etc. built to celebrate a famous person or event

motorhome /ˈməʊtəhəʊm/ *n* a large motor vehicle designed for people to live and sleep in when they are travelling

Must Tells /ˈmʌst telz/ *n* important information or interesting stories that a tour guide should tell about a famous place or person

national park /ˌnæʃnəl ˈpɑːk/ *n* an area of land that is protected by the government for people to visit because of its natural beauty

niche /niːʃ/ /nɪtʃ/ *n* an opportunity to sell a product for which there is limited demand, but which few or no other companies produce or offer

olive oil /ˌɒlɪv ˈɔɪl/ *n* oil made from olives used in cooking and on salads

overbookings /ˌəʊvəˈbʊkɪŋz/ *n* a situation in which more rooms have been reserved than there are places available

overcast /ˌəʊvəˈkɑːst/ *adj* (used about the sky) grey and covered with clouds

panoramic tour /pænəˌræmɪk ˈtʊə(r)/ *n* a short tour on a coach or a boat in which you see all the most important sights of a city, town, etc.

parade /pəˈreɪd/ *n* a public celebration of a special day or event, usually with bands in the streets and decorated vehicles

pax /pæks/ *n* passengers / people

pay TV /ˌpeɪ tiː ˈviː/ *n* a system in some hotels in which you pay extra money to watch particular TV channels or films

payment slip /ˈpeɪmənt slɪp/ *n* a small piece of paper given to a customer to show that they have paid their bill

pedal boat /ˈpedl bəʊt/ *n* a small pleasure boat that you operate by pushing pedals with your feet

pepper /ˈpepə(r)/ *n* a hollow fruit, usually red, green, or yellow, that is eaten as a vegetable either raw or cooked

period costume /ˈpɪəriəd ˌkɒstjuːm/ *n* clothes worn so that you look like somebody from a particular period in the past

pick-up /ˈpɪk ʌp/ *n* the place where a person or thing is collected from

pitch /pɪtʃ/ *n* a space where you can put a tent or a **motorhome** on a campsite

pork /pɔːk/ *n* meat from a pig

posture /ˈpɒstʃə(r)/ *n* the position in which you hold your body when standing or sitting

pottery /ˈpɒtəri/ *n* 1. pots, dishes, etc. made with clay (= a heavy, sticky earth) that is baked in an oven, especially when they are made by hand 2. the skill of making pottery

prawn /prɔːn/ *n* a small shellfish with ten legs and a tail that you can eat and which turns pink when cooked

pre-book /ˌpriːˈbʊk/ *v* to arrange to have something such as a room, seat, or ticket in advance

presentation /ˌpreznˈteɪʃn/ *n* a meeting at which a new product, an idea, etc. is shown to a group of people

procession /prəˈseʃn/ *n* a line of people or vehicles that moves along slowly, especially as part of a ceremony

product launch /ˈprɒdʌkt lɔːntʃ/ *n* an event at which a new product is presented to the public for the first time

projector / digital projector /prəˈdʒektə(r)/ /ˌdɪdʒɪtl prəˈdʒektə(r)/ *n* a device that is used to show photographs or films on a screen

public relations (PR) /ˌpʌblɪk rɪˈleɪʃnz/ *n* the activity of communicating with people in order to create and maintain a good impression of an organization

pulses /ˈpʌlsɪz/ *n* the seeds of some plants that are eaten as food, for example peas and lentils

quiz /kwɪz/ *n* a competition or game in which people have to answer questions to test their knowledge

ramp /ræmp/ *n* a slope at the entrance to a door, building, etc. that allows people using **wheelchairs** to enter or leave easily

ranger /ˈreɪndʒə(r)/ *n* a person whose job is to take care of a park, a forest, or an area of countryside

rash /ræʃ/ *n* an area of red spots on a person's skin, caused by an illness or an **allergic** reaction

recorded information /reˌkɔːdɪd ˌɪnfəˈmeɪʃn/ *n* a telephone service that you can call for information about something

re-enactment /ˌriː ɪˈnæktmənt/ *n* the act of repeating the actions of a famous event from the past

register /ˈredʒɪstə(r)/ *v* 1. to record a guest's name, address, etc. when they arrive at a hotel 2. to show or record an amount of money on a machine

registration card /ˌredʒɪˈstreɪʃn kɑːd/ *n* a short form that you fill in when you register at a hotel

relief driver /rɪˈliːf ˌdraɪvə(r)/ *n* a driver that replaces another driver when they have finished working for the day or when they are sick

renovate /ˈrenəveɪt/ *v* to repair, paint, etc. an old building, so that it is in good condition again

represent /ˌreprɪˈzent/ *v* to be a **symbol** of something

retired person /rɪˈtaɪəd ˌpɜːsn/ *n* somebody who no longer works because they have reached a particular age

roof-rack /ˈruːf ˌræk/ *n* a metal frame fixed to the roof of a car and used for carrying bags, cases, and other large objects

room rack /ruːm ˈræk/ *n* a computer screen or a board showing which rooms are available in a hotel

rooming list /ˈruːmɪŋ lɪst/ *n* a piece of paper with the names of all the passengers travelling on a tour and the hotel room they are each staying in

routine task /ruːˌtiːn ˈtɑːsk/ *n* a piece of work that you must regularly do as part of your job

rush hour /ˈrʌʃ ˌaʊə(r)/ *n* the time when the roads are full of traffic and trains are crowded because people are travelling to or from work

sausage /ˈsɒsɪdʒ/ *n* a mixture of finely chopped meat in a long tube of skin

scuba diving /'sku:bə daɪvɪŋ/ *n* swimming underwater using special breathing equipment including a container of air carried on your back

sculpture /'skʌlptʃə(r)/ *n* a work of art that is a solid figure, made by shaping wood, stone, metal, etc.

seafront /'si:frʌnt/ *n* the part of a town facing the sea

seasonal /'si:zənl/ *adj* happening or needed during a particular season (= part of the year)

sense of humour /sens əv 'hju:mə(r)/ *n* the ability to tell jokes and laugh at things that are amusing

shower /'ʃaʊə(r)/ *n* a short period of rain

sign /saɪn/ *v* to write your name on a document to show that you agree with what it says

sign language /'saɪn ˌlæŋgwɪdʒ/ *n* a system of communication used by **deaf** people, using hand actions rather than spoken words

signage /'saɪnɪdʒ/ *n* signs that give instructions or directions to the public

signature /'sɪgnətʃə(r)/ *n* the act of **signing** your name on a document; your name, as it is written when signing a document

snorkelling /'snɔ:kəlɪŋ/ *n* swimming underwater using a snorkel (= a short tube that you breathe through)

socialize /'səʊʃəlaɪz/ *v* to meet and talk informally with other people

sore /sɔ:(r)/ *adj* (used about a part of your body) painful, and often red, because of infection, injury, etc.

spices /'spaɪsɪz/ *n* powders or seeds from plants that are used in cooking to give food a strong smell or **flavour**

stand /stænd/ *n* a table or vertical structure where a company displays its products at an **exhibition**

starter /'stɑ:tə(r)/ *n* a small **dish** of food served before the main course in a meal

statue /'stætʃu:/ *n* a large stone or metal figure of a person, animal, etc.

stewed /stju:d/ *adj* cooked slowly in liquid in a closed dish

storm /stɔ:m/ *n* a period of heavy rain, strong winds, etc., usually with **thunder** and lightning

stuffed /stʌft/ *adj* (used about something you eat) filled with something else

sunburn /'sʌnbɜ:n/ *n* the condition of having red skin that is **sore**, caused by spending too much time in the sun

sunny intervals /ˌsʌni 'ɪntəvlz/ *n* short periods of sunshine between periods of rain or cloudy weather

survey /'sɜ:veɪ/ *n* an investigation of the opinions of a particular group of people, usually by asking them questions

swipe /swaɪp/ *v* to pass a plastic card, such as a credit card, through a special machine that is able to read the information stored on it

swollen /'swəʊlən/ *adj* (used about a part of the body) larger than normal because of an injury, infection, etc.

symbol /'sɪmbl/ *n* a sign or image that has a specific meaning

sympathy /'sɪmpəθi/ *n* showing that you understand and care about somebody's problems

(fuel) tank /tæŋk/ *n* a container inside the body of a car that holds the petrol

taste /teɪst/ *n* a small quantity of food or drink that you try in order to see what it is like

taxi rank /'tæksi ræŋk/ *n* a place where taxis park while they are waiting for passengers

teenager /'ti:neɪdʒə(r)/ *n* a person aged between thirteen and nineteen

teleconferencing /ˌteli'kɒnfərənsɪŋ/ *n* having a meeting at which members are in different places and speak to each other using telephone and video connections

theatre-style /'θɪətə staɪl/ *adj* (used about seats) arranged in rows with all the seats facing towards the front where the speaker stands

third-party liability /ˌθɜ:d ˌpɑ:ti ˌlaɪə'bɪləti/ *n* car insurance that only pays for damage / injury that you do to another driver, their passengers, or their car

throat /θrəʊt/ *n* the passage in the neck that food and air pass through

thunder /'θʌndə(r)/ *n* a loud noise that accompanies a flash of lightning in a **storm**

tip /tɪp/ *v* to give a small extra amount of money (= a tip) to somebody, such as a waiter, who has done a job or service for you

tone /təʊn/ *n* the quality of your voice and the emotion this expresses

toothache /'tu:θeɪk/ *n* a pain in your teeth or in a tooth

Top Visual Priority /tɒp ˌvɪʒuəl praɪ'ɒrəti/ *n* the main sight that a tour guide must show to people on a tour

touch screen /'tʌtʃ skri:n/ *n* a computer screen that allows you change what you see by touching particular areas on it

tour manager /'tʊə ˌmænɪdʒə(r)/ *n* a person whose job involves organizing tours, including managing the tour guides, arranging accommodation, etc.

tourist information centre (TIC) /ti: aɪ 'si:/ /ˌtʊərɪst ˌɪnfə'meɪʃn ˌsentə(r)/ *n* an office in a city or large town that gives information to people visiting that area about accommodation, places to visit, etc.

transit lounge /'trænzɪt ˌlaʊndʒ/ *n* a place in an airport where passengers who are changing planes can wait for their next plane

trendy /'trendi/ *adj* fashionable

uniform /'ju:nɪfɔ:m/ *n* a set of clothes worn by everyone who works for a particular company

unwell /ʌn'wel/ *adj* ill / sick

update /ˌʌp'deɪt/ *v* to add the most recent information to a set of records

upgrade /ˌʌp'greɪd/ *v* to get a better quality car, plane seat, etc. usually by paying extra money

upset /ʌpˈset/ *adj* (used about your stomach) having an illness that makes you feel sick or have **diarrhoea**

U-shaped /ˈjuː ʃeɪpt/ *adj* having a curved shape with straight sides, like the letter *U*

value for money /ˌvæljuː fə ˈmʌni/ *n* a measure of how good something is when you consider its price and compare it with other similar products or services

variable /ˈveəriəbl/ *adj* changing or tending to change

videoconferencing /ˌvɪdiəʊˈkɒnfərənsɪŋ/ *n* having a meeting at which members are in different places and see and speak to each other using video connections

video-gaming /ˈvɪdiəʊ ˌɡeɪmɪŋ/ *n* playing electronic games in which you press buttons to control images on a screen

VIP /ˌviː aɪ ˈpiː/ *n* an important person who is treated in a special way (abbreviation for 'very important person')

visual impairment /ˈvɪʒuəl ɪmˌpeəmənt/ *n* a physical condition which prevents you from seeing normally

voucher /ˈvaʊtʃə(r)/ *n* a paper document that shows that a guest has already paid for a room

walk-in /ˈwɔːk ɪn/ *n* a **chance guest**

walkway /ˈwɔːkweɪ/ *n* a passage or path for walking along

warden /ˈwɔːdn/ *n* a person whose job involves guarding or looking after a place, such as a park

waxworks /ˈwækswɜːks/ *n* models of people, particularly famous people, made of wax

weaving /wiːvɪŋ/ *n* the activity of making **cloth**, carpets, etc. by crossing threads over and under each other by hand or on a machine

welcome /ˈwelkəm/ *n* something that you do or say to somebody when they arrive to show that you are happy to see them

wheelchair /ˈwiːltʃeə(r)/ *n* a special chair with wheels, used to move around by people who cannot walk

wi-fi /ˈwaɪ faɪ/ *adj* using a system for sending data over computer networks that uses radio waves instead of wires

windscreen /ˈwɪndskriːn/ *n* the window across the front of a car or other vehicle

woodcarving /ˈwʊdkɑːvɪŋ/ *n* the activity of shaping wood into designs or figures, using a sharp tool

yogurt (also yoghurt) /ˈjɒɡət/ *n* a thick white liquid food that is eaten cold and is made by adding bacteria to milk and often flavoured with fruit

OXFORD
UNIVERSITY PRESS

Great Clarendon Street, Oxford OX2 6DP

Oxford University Press is a department of the University of Oxford.
It furthers the University's objective of excellence in research, scholarship,
and education by publishing worldwide in

Oxford New York

Auckland Cape Town Dar es Salaam Hong Kong Karachi
Kuala Lumpur Madrid Melbourne Mexico City Nairobi
New Delhi Shanghai Taipei Toronto

With offices in

Argentina Austria Brazil Chile Czech Republic France Greece
Guatemala Hungary Italy Japan Poland Portugal Singapore
South Korea Switzerland Thailand Turkey Ukraine Vietnam

OXFORD and OXFORD ENGLISH are registered trade marks of
Oxford University Press in the UK and in certain other countries

© Oxford University Press 2007

ISBN: 978 0 19 455103 8

Printed and bound in Italy by Rotolito Lombarda S.p.A.

ACKNOWLEDGEMENTS

*The authors and publisher are grateful to those who have given permission to reproduce the
following extracts and adaptations of copyright material:*

p25 Text from Kontrapunkt. Used with permission.

p30 Extract from 'Resort Representative' job profile http://www.learndirect-
advice.co.uk/helpwithyourcareer/jobprofiles/profiles/profile333/. Reproduced with
permission from Learndirect and Ufi Ltd.

p33 Extract from Natives.co.uk – 'the Season Workers' website'. Reproduced with
permission.

p92 from p230 of *Vocational A-LEVEL Travel and Tourism Options Second Edition* by Ray
Youell. With kind permission from Pearson Education Ltd.

p42 Extracts from www.cntower.ca Copyright of Canada Lands Company CLC
Limited. Reproduced with permission.

p64 Festa del Redentore from *The Mini Rough Guide to Mediterranean Festivals*.
Reproduced with permission.

p66 Golden Gate National Parks Conservancy. www.parksconservancy.co.uk
Reproduced with permission.

p68–69 Extract from the Cambridge alumni travel programme. Reproduced with
kind permission from ACE Study Tours.

p69 & 132 Mark Hempshell: *Getting a Job in Travel and Tourism*, Oxford: How to Books,
3rd edition, 1998 p48–49; ISBN: 1 85703 268 3

p84–85 Reprinted from *Niche Tourism* by Maria Novelli. 'Alternative Tourism
Development' p9 © 2004, with permission from Elsevier.

p86 From Photoventures. www.photoventures.net.

p98 'Combining Business with Pleasure' Page 256 from *Business Travel* by Davidson &
Cope. Reproduced with kind permission from Pearson Education Ltd.

*Although every effort has been made to trace and contact copyright holders before publication,
this has not been possible in some cases. We apologize for any apparent infringement of
copyright and if notified, the publisher will be pleased to rectify any errors or omissions at the
earliest opportunity.*

Sources: p11 Rough Guide to South Africa; p15 www.jobsinhotels.co.uk; p48
www.ratztamara.com/rural.pdf; p50 www.countrysideaccess.gov.uk; p71
www.stga.co.uk Scottish Tour Guides Association

*The authors and publisher are grateful to the following for their permission to reproduce
photographs and illustrative material:* Alamy Images pp4 (welcome banner/M. Timothy
O'Keefe), 5 (flower/Bjorn Holland), 8 (Ford Ka/Motoring Picture Library), 8 (Ford
Fiesta/Motoring Picture Library), 8 (Dodge Stratus/Carphotos), 10 (passport stamp/
Sbastien Baussais), 20 (leafleats/Chris Howes/Wild Places Photography), 20 (tourist
information office/Carsten Flieger), 24 (football stadium/rimmer), 26 (visitor
information centre/Chris Fredriksson), 28 (holiday rep greeting tourists/Rob
Rayworth, basketball game/KCS-Stockphotos, camping site in rain/Alan Oliver),
30 (mobile phone/Nick Emm), 36 (bigos/Profimedia Inernational s.r.o., Mexico flag/
Eric Nathan), 39 (fish and chips/foodfolio), 44 (conservation work/Janna Bilska, ski
resort/Graham Lawrence, basket weaving/Mark Pink), 45 (young man/Jennie Hart),
46 (villa/Mathew Lodge), 48 (weaving/Bill Lyons), 50 (village on water/Terry
Whittaker), 60 (beefeater/Jon Arnold Images, park ranger/Visions of America LCC,
gallery guide/Alex Serge, guide in the pyramids/John James), 74 (coach/Motoring
Picture Library), 76 (rural hotel/Bramwellslocker), 84 (plane spotter/Colin Underhill,
mining/Greenshoots Communicaions), 88 (man in wheelchair/Sandra Baker), 96
(video projector/Tony Codoza), 97 (pen/Mick Broughton), 98 (Mirage Hotel/Jon
Arnold Images), 100 (Durban/PCL), 104 (hair dryer/GoGo Images Corporation, ice
machine/Seth Smoot), 107 (beach/Robert Harding Picture Library); BAA Aviation
Picture Library p20 (information area in an airport/David J. Osborn); Corbis cover
(Jutta Klee), pp5 (Singapore at night/Jose Fuste Raga), 9 (car exhaust/Jose Lius Pelaez,
Inc.), 11 (Table Mountain/Onne van der Wal), 12 (DND sign/William Whitehurst,
businesswoman in hotel/Jed Share and Kaoru), 14 (key card/George Diebold/Veer),
17 (scales/Bloomimage), 19 (balloon/John Hicks), 20 (call centre/Tim Pannell), 22
(beach huts/Steven Vidler/Eurasia Press), 23 (pedestrian crossing sign/Don Hammond/
Design Pics), 24 (Richard Klune/Albert Docks, Liverpool), 26 (Legoland/Stephan
Puncher/dpa, Copenhagen/ML Sinibaldi), 28 (couple on beach/Paul Steel), 32 (ski
instructor/Mike Powell), 33 (ski slope/Adam Woolfitt/Robert Harding World Imagery),
36 (kebab/Rainer Holz), 40 (Turkish food/Lawrence Manning), 44 (tourists and carpet
weaver/S. Hammid/zefa, golfer/Stefan Schuetz, rock climber/Anne-Marie Weber,
bird watcher/Larry Williams, Greek tour guide/Mika/zefa), 45 (salt lake/Blaine
Harrington III), 48 (brewing/Owen Franken, water mill/Hubert Stadler), 50
(basket with silkworms/Nevada Wier), 54 (buddhist temple/Diege Azubel/epa),
67 (St Petersburg/Bo Zaunders), 68 (ruins in Libya/Bob Kirst, sea lion/Paul Souders),
73 (Green Park/Jim Richardson), 74 (tartan kilts/Robert Holmes), 76 (Las Vegas at
night/Grafton Marshall Smith, beach house/Dan Forer/Beatworks, people in
nightclub/Randy Faris, children's activities/Tom Gill, scuba diving/Hans Neleman/
zefa, spa/Simon Marcus, video games/C. Devan/zefa), 84 (cosmetic surgery
consultation/T&L/Image Point FR), 92 (airline check-in/Jon Feingersh), 96 (video
conference/Steve Chenn), 98 (Westin hotel/Jon Butchofsky-Houser), 101 (hotel lobby/
Randy Faris), 102 (rugs/Carl & Ann Purcell), 111 (guacho festival/Andres Stapff/
Reuters), 117 (water festival/STR/epa); Getty Images pp4 (conference welcome desk/
Riser, Las Vegas sign/Steven Puetzer/Stone), 6 (namaste/IZA Stock), 12 (car outside
hotel/Car Culture, people in hotel lobby/Romilly Lockyer/Image Bank), 18 (hotel
staff/Siri Stafford/Stone), 19 (concierge/Frederic Lucano/Taxi), 23 (footpath/Nick
Dolding/Taxi, Cavern club/John Pratt/Hulton Archive), 30 (meeting/Reza Estakhrian/
Stone), 32 (chalet/Ellen Rooney/Robert Harding World Imagery), 34 (bell boy/
Michael Coglaintry/ImageBank), 40 (Turkey nightlife/Scott R Barbour), 44 (temple
entrance/A. Witte/C. Mahaney/Photographer's Choice), 48 (pottery wheel/David
Hume Kennerly/Reportage, paddy field/Peter Adams/Image Bank), 54 (Hong Kong
Harbour/Neil Emerson/Robert Harding World Imagery), 61 (water park/Jason
Hawkes/Photographer's Choice), 63 (Notre Dame/Images Etc Ltd/Photographer's
Choice), 66 (Alcatraz island/Tom Palva/Taxi), 70 (opera house/Foto World/Image
Bank), 76 (aqua aerobics/Zac Macaulay/Image Bank, fitness centre/Lori Adamski-
Peek/Taxi, rollerblading/Chris M. Rogers/Image Bank, swimming/Frank Bauer/
Stone), 80 (portrait of young man/Dimitri Verits/Photonica), 84 (hospital/Brand
Wilson/Image Bank), 90 (binoculars/Aleruaro/SambaPhoto), 92 (catering/Romilly
Lockyer/Image Bank), 96 (man with flipchart/Max Oppenheim/Image Bank), 96
(laptop/Justin Sullivan), 102 (young man/Seth Joel/Photographer's Choice); Jupiter
Images p4 (welcome sign on bed/FoodPix); Lonely Planet Images pp20 (people
reading information point/Richard Cummins), 40 (Turkish delight/John Hay);
Masterfile pp42 (Toronto/Scott Tysick), 76 (magician), 76 (pedal boat/George Shelley),
84 (rock climber/Brad Wrobleski), 84 (couple on holiday/Steve Prezant), 95 (New
Dehli/Jeremy Woodhouse); OUP pp5 (Singapore flag/Stockbyte, smiling mouth), 26
(Copenhagen Mermaid), 30 (clipboard), 36 (flags/Stockbyte), 62 (Arc du Triomphe),
73 (Tower Bridge), 76 (windsurfing), 90 (globe), 97 (beach, boy, bear, peach, pear);
Photolibrary.com pp24 (Eurodisney/Chad Ehlers/Nordicphotos, Liverpool street/
JTB Photo), 28 (ski school/Christian Arnal/Photononstop), 36 (prawn cocktail/David
Prince/Foodpix, sushi/Foodpix, bread wrap/Bill Bettencourt/Foodpix), 37 (bread/
Rosenfeld/Mauritius Die Bildagentur GmbH, chocolate/Foodfolio/Imagestate Ltd),
39 (chicken cutlet/Brian Hagiwara/Foodpix, tagine/Tim Hill, Greek salad/Michael
Pohuski/Foodpix), 112 (Jerez festival/JTB Photo); Pierre d'Alancaisez pp12 (diary),
71 (click counter); Punchstock pp4 (airport terminal sign/Creatas, airport greeting/
Digital Vision), 15 (receptionist/ImageSource), 20 (hotel information/Banana Stock),
23 (baby changing sign/Peter Dazeley/Photographer's Choice), 36 (curry/Photodisc),
44 (young man with backpack/Digital Vision, young man/Blend), 48 (orchard/Digital
Vision), 64 (Il Redentore, Venice/Radius), 69 (tour rep on coach/Digital Vision), 76
(tv/Digital Vision, Nevada/Digital Vision), 80 (children's entertainer/Stockbyte),
82 (young woman with microphone/Digital Vision), 90 (conference registration/
Stockbyte), 92 (trade show/Stockbyte), 103 (check-in/Photodisc); Rex Features
p98 (Chelsea Hotel); Roger Reynonds/Photoventures p86; Spectrum Stock pp5
(people in outdoor café/Murat Ayranci), 37 (fishing boat/age fotostock), 66 (Alcatraz
prison interior/Geri Lavrov), 70 (young woman, Odessa steps/Silvio Fiore), 76 (card
table), 79 (Las Vegas/Brian Lawrence), 102 (Azadi Tower, Tehran); StockFood pp39
(harira/Barbara Lutterbeck, moussaka/Peter Rees); Tips Images Ltd. p64 (Fiesta del
Redentore, Venice/Mark Edward Smith).

Illustrations by: Maria Colino at Folio (customer care cartoons), Tim Kahane, Russell
Tate at Apple (maps).

*The authors and publisher would like to thank the many teachers, schools, and institutions
who assisted in the development of this title, in particular:* Daniel García, María del Mar
Fernandez & Amelia Valiente, Hotel Silken Monumental, Oviedo, Spain; David
Spoor, The Big Sleep Hotel, Cardiff, UK; Verónica Quintero, Cosmo Entertainment,
Mallorca; María García López, Oviedo, Spain; Sofia da Costa, Hesperia Tower Hotel,
Barcelona, Spain; the staff and students of the Escuela Universitaria de Turismo de
Asturias, Oviedo, Spain.